Literature of the American West
William Kittredge, General Editor

Other books by Linda Hussa

Poetry
Where the Wind Lives (Reno, Nev., 1995)
Ride the Silence (Layton, Utah, 1994)

Nonfiction
Diary of a Cow Camp Cook (Cedarville, Calif., 1990)

Lige Langston

University of Oklahoma Press

Norman

Lige Langston

Sweet Iron

Linda Hussa

With best Wishes
Linda Hussa
- 2000 -

Lige Langston: Sweet Iron
is Volume 4 in the Literature of the
American West series.

Library of Congress Cataloging-in-Publication Data

Hussa, Linda.
   Lige Langston: Sweet Iron / Linda Hussa
      p.   cm.   – (Literature of the American West; v. 4)
   ISBN 0-8061-3109-8 (alk. paper)
      1. Langston, Henry Elijah, 1908–1987.   2. Ranchers–Nevada–
   Washoe County–Biography.   3. Pioneers–Nevada–Washoe
   County–Biography.   4. Ranch Life–Nevada–Washoe County–
   History–20th century.   5. Frontier and pioneer life–Nevada–
   Washoe County.   6. Washoe County (Nev.)–Social life and
   customs.   7. Washoe County (Nev.)–Biography.   I. Title.
   II. Series.
   F847.W3H97 1998
   979.3'5503'092–dc21
   [B]   98-39709
                                                                    CIP

The paper in this book meets the guidelines for permanence and
durability of the Committee on Production Guidelines for Book
Longevity of the Council on Library Resources, Inc. ♾

Published by the University of Oklahoma Press, Norman, Publish-
ing Division of the University. All rights reserved. Manufactured in
the U.S.A.

Book design by Wesley B. Tanner/ Passim Editions, Ann Arbor

1 2 3 4 5 6 7 8 9 10

In memory of
Henry Elijah Langston and Lee G. Vinson,
and to John Hussa

The old-timers who made bits set a great deal of importance on the type of steel that went into the mouthpiece. They were very careful to use only "sweet" iron. Nor would they forge a mouthpiece with any coal other than mesquite charcoal. Vaqueros believed that a bit is not good until it has been tempered and sweetened by the heat of the horse's mouth.

Arnold R. Rojas, *These Were the Vaqueros*

I knew of Lige Langston before we met in 1971. In a small town there is time for stories to reach everyone. Lige didn't talk about himself directly. It wasn't his way. He braided himself in stories of ranch life in the early 1900s, horses he learned from, and men he rode with, while he worked rawhide in his basement. I had to be alert to catch the silent things that were the most important. After Lige died, friends and family laid on other strands. The braiding became richer, intricate, smooth.

He returns to me in their faces, their manner when they speak of him. And I find notes, letters, articles in my mailbox as I might find a hawk feather on the sod and braid it in a buttonhole as mine. His memory pricks me to remember him – and men like him – who rode rough horses to care for cattle on a wild land. They needed work to do and comrades who understood what it took to master the work in days when it counted to be honest and resolute and a friend someone could lean their life against. They stayed apart from townsfolk denned up like prairie dogs in the stern persuasion of electric lights, away from a wall's embrace or well-meaning warmth. They wanted an unbranded place.

When they were lonely they rode to town and filled up fast, self-generous and unashamed, only to be awakened by a breath in the short grass. They dressed in the dark, slipped the blind from the bridle, and returned – monks of the cold desert.

The desert is part of his story but she must be imagined. She is a collector. She absorbs the earth's tremors. She endured a 3,000-year drought and can wait for a loving rain. She keeps a secret longer than anyone. Distance and horizons are her best features and she commands light in both value and range. She can teach anything that must be known. Silence is her healing voice.

Lige Langston

My dad used to say Lige sat straighter in a saddle than anyone. As far away as you could see riders, you could pick out Lige.

Lavelle Stevens Dollarhide, rancher

My husband's grandmother left us a huge meat platter, large enough to embrace a twenty-pound roast, a leg of lamb from an old-cropper, a whole ham, or two dozen quail nested in rice. The sides of the platter scoop upward gracefully to hold rich meat broth. Her platter reminds me of Duck Flat, Nevada – of Lige. Hand-painted beneath the gold rim before the final glaze was fired is a lacy pattern, and mountains design the rim of the Flat, where Lige was born.

Henry Elijah "Lige" Langston, 1908-1987

Lige worked alone, broke horses for my dad when I was a kid. These were broncos, some of 'em five-, six-year-olds, maybe seven. Smart. Strong. Not used to people. Never been halter broke. Never been handled. Wild as any wild animal. Bite, kick, strike, they'd do it all, and mean it.

Lige'd run one into the round corral and I'd watch through the poles. Two fighters sparring, the energy just snapped between 'em! One of 'em was tryin' to do things right, quiet as he could. The other was fightin' for his life – that's how the horse looked at it. You gotta remember, his free life was about to change forever and he didn't want any part of it. First off, Lige had to rope that wild snake. When he touched the horse its whole body would quiver. It'd jerk away, go down on its knees, to avoid his hand. Lige'd get the hobbles on, tie up a hind leg, saddle him, get on and off, on and off with him tied up, off balance. This handlin' 'em, bein' that close, touchin' 'em, did a lot to their mind. Can't you just imagine?

Then Lige took off the foot rope but left the hobbles. Got on and off some more. He'd get down, pull the slip

knot on the hobbles, and step on. The bronco hadn't figured out yet he was free, but when Lige made him take
that first step, it could get western! He'd either run
scared or go to buckin'. Lige was tryin' to teach him not
to buck and start thinkin'. The horse had to learn to give
himself to the man and this was lesson number one. No
two horses were the same. Some of 'em wanted to get
along, others wanted a brawl, just like people. Lige did
what it took to reach their mind. If they were kind, he
was kind. But he could be rough if that's what they
wanted.

When Lige felt like he could handle the horse outside
he'd take the poles down and that's where they'd go. Like
as not the colt would pitch it to him again out there in
the yard and the quirt would come down, pop! on that
bronco's nose, to get his head up. Off they'd go in the
dust, 'cross the country. I'd curl up in the grass by the
corral and take a nap. Pretty soon, here he'd come ridin'
back. He'd unsaddle that one and get himself another. It
would go on like that till supper.

That year built for me on Lige ridin' broncos, turnin'
'em into saddle horses. Mom had the good sense to let it
happen.

Bill Cockrell, rancher

Lige borrowed Dick Scott's new '38 Ford coupe to take Francine to Reno to get married. On the way home they missed a bridge and tore the car up. They were able to get home but it was wrecked! That same winter Lige wanted to buy a light little saddle I had for Francine. Said he'd give me twenty dollars, so I let him take it. He didn't have any money. It went on about a year and I told him he had to give me the money or the saddle. He brought the saddle back . . . didn't have twenty dollars. 'Course, that all happened before he married Etta.

Dick Winnop, *trucker*

Lige was forever playing wild horses when we were children. It was the only game that interested him. When I was about three and Lige six, some people came up to visit Mom. She met them in San Francisco when she first came out west from Louisiana. Mom said they seemed dumbfounded by the drive up the desert and our place on the Flat, but they recovered and asked to see the children. They especially wanted to see "the girl." So Mom called and called, but I didn't come. They went out lookin' and finally found me. I was the horse. I was tied to the hitchrail in the barn. Those city folks were shocked. I don't think Mom ever heard from them again.

Jessie Langston Holmes

Part 1

A horse's nature changes three times
from the starting ride up until he is a
finished horse –

Lige pulled his pickup off the pavement on a breaking ridge, Mail Box Hill, and turned the engine off. He sat quietly looking south, out his window. I watched the miniature quirt he'd braided from rawhide scraps swing from the keyring and when the swaying stopped, the leather popper on the end pointed down – a divining rod signaling this was the spot. We got out and leaned against his side of the truck facing into afternoon sun. Lige slowly walked my vision around the blue gray basin of Duck Flat as he pointed out Rye Patch, the Cambron Place, the Mason Place, the Powell Place.

Pencil thin poplars survived the harsh climate of this high desert basin. But most of the homesteads had melted back into the alkali dust leaving no sign of what held them to the long curving basin for a time. Yet they still populated Lige's memory. In an isolated valley like Duck Flat remembered neighbors could become near kin.

His outstretched arm stopped on a bend near Tuledad Canyon. I knew the place that clung to his eyes was his family homestead. The tin roofs of house and barn rode the heat of the desert afternoon. Shadows underlined it all. Corral and pasture fencing broke the random march of brush with dark lines in a country that did not move in lines. It was all miles away but totally visible. I could almost guess where the clothesline was strung. A flash of light told me about the windmill. The tree on the southwest corner soothed a room where a baby could nap. But the carriage of the house was east, where the sun spoke first and walking to the barn would be walking into its certain greeting.

With a slight nod he said, "That's the Langston Place."

He waited while I slipped into my side of the truck. The little quirt turned just as he might urge a balky colt. The blue pickup responded. We drove toward the ranch on the west side of the Flat.

*Pa and Mom filed on Duck Flat. All the
good country was taken up.*

Jessie

I had seen mammoth bones big around as small trees, dense
as stone, that Davey Grove dug up at his windmill and carried
home to his yard. I knew of a Clovis point an archeologist
scooped up in the dunes. I had crossed the Flat when rare spring
rains flooded every low place and Lost Creek threatened to take
out the road, and felt a curiosity about this thumbprint, Duck
Flat. But now, learning that this twenty or so mile curve of sagebrush and swale was where Lige was born and raised, I wanted
to know more.

Mary Austin said, "Nevada is geology by day, astronomy at
night." The historic record is as complex as the definition of the
Great Basin, but the geological phenomena that shaped it
shaped Duck Flat. One of the most significant was the subsi-
dence of tablelands as the Sierras, Cascades, and Warners
wrenched up out of the western plateaus in a mountain wall
that became the western boundary of the Great Basin. The
mountains formed a barricade that absorbs or deflects warm
Pacific storms. The country within the rain shadow changed
from a temperate woodland into a high cold desert. Second, a
massive explosion ripped open Hell's Canyon and sucked the
Snake, Bear, and Owyhee rivers into the Columbia Gorge and
denied the inland sea of the Great Basin their waters forever.
Strandlines of that ancient sea are plainly etched on the eastern
face of the valley. The water dropped and held, dropped and
held until it slowly dried up. Aboriginal campsites responded to

the ebb and flow. The litter of their lives works loose from soil and stone.

It's a basin in a series of Nevada basins. A topography map of the state looks like a marcelled hairdo of the '30s, and this particular finger dip or wave is called the Flat. Coming at it from the north canyon, the road slants up Mail Box Ridge. The curtain of the hill drops and the Flat – turning in a long sweep of distance – is the color of human skin. Few traces of man flirt my mind away.

Mountains stand out on the horizon as I turn with the compass. Fox Mountain is to the east. A steep canyon climbs out over Squaw Valley Mountain to the south. In the west, the South Warner Mountains lift abruptly above the Coppersmiths in juniper-covered hills and then break over into the sister basin of the Madeline Plains. And north, the road is direct into Surprise Valley, just across the border, in California.

Surprise Valley is a larger fertile valley with four settlements along the Warner Mountains. In the early 1900s homesteaders on the Flat were within a day's ride of Eagleville's school, church, store, bank, blacksmith, lumber mill, and flour mill. The Rodero Club served Sunday supper, dances were held in the Cambron building, Louie Grove ran a garage, and Doc Gibson had an office in the back of his bar. Cedarville, another day's ride north at the mouth of Cedar Canyon, is where the main road leaves the valley to the county seat in Alturas. Pegnellis's Tinshop and Lamb's Hardware were at the crossroads. There was an ice cream parlor in the Meredith Building. Gay Delmas sold candy, fruits, and vegetables. Her store also served as a freight and express office, and she owned the Gluck Movie House. True

Hapgood ran a garage on the south end of town; Posey Green's was on the north end. Valentine Jaurena and his brother Lucio had a paddleball court and cardroom in the loft above the old granary. James Wylie's law office was alongside the post office, William McCombs's wagon and cabinet shop out back. Hope Ledford had a bakery. There was an apple dryer that later was used as a morgue, five hotels, a dozen bars, and three general merchandise stores – Johnston & Sons, Inc., Cressler & Bonner, and Denehy's Store, which advertised it had "Everything for Everybody." Lake City split the distance to Fort Bidwell, at the far north end of the seventy-mile-long valley. Fort Bidwell was supported by the army post until the turn of the century, boom and bust gold mines on Bidwell Mountain, a brewery, and the largest Paiute rancheria north of Pyramid Lake. One constable kept the peace but each town had its own jail.

Duck Flat is higher and drier. Moisture trickles from the surrounding winter peaks, feeding ribbons of grass in every canyon as it seeps toward Duck Lake at the north end. Floating on the surface are pelicans, mud hens, honkers, brandts, mallards, teal, swans when it's filled up; people haying or the scatter of feeding cattle when it's not.

Most of the state is designated as semiarid or arid and stockmen have come to expect little live water. The occasional spring swells up a fringe of willow, Great Basin rye, aspen, and cottonwoods. Obsidian chips indicate a reliable spring, perhaps centuries old. Trails that meander across the Flat take a direct line when they near such an oasis, resembling a spiderweb, or the spokes of a wheel that embrace at the hub. Prints ring the damp sand with a necklace of its lovers. So far from the moon yet it is here she comes to bathe.

These Nevada basin people shared grazing and water. They helped as neighbors do. They left their names behind and their stories draped like the sagging fence wire that can trip a foot and make someone remember.

Brief insanity settled on the Flat in the early 1900s like a blanket of fog the Paiutes call *pogonip*, which hugs down for long dreary weeks in January, and snow, if there is any, freezes into sugar, squeaks and kicks aside but cannot melt a drop of water. Three men named Sweet homesteaded a place that became known as Rye Patch, and one, or all three at once, dreamed a scheme to get irrigation water to their dry fields by tunneling through the foothills to drain Son-of-a-bitch Lake into a pipe. They laid tracks and ran coal carts into the yawning hole they disappeared into every morning. Would one alone have carried the plan past whimsy without the other two to punctuate the possibility with the ring of pick and blister-raising no. 2 shovel? They gave it up but their story dug in to stay.

There were other flights of fancy: a chicken and egg ranch, a bar and store at Sunkist, a goat farm, a lime kiln in the canyon, a brothel at Readerville, hogs and turkeys. But mainly the homesteaders were stockmen: cattle and horses. They were the usual mix of nationality and integrity that show up when the initial investment is plain old hard work.

People have been passing through the Flat for eleven thousand years, sheltering from the harshness, both heat and bitter cold. They shed like winter hair and fly on the spring winds or twist down deep as sage roots and take on the same stubborn look. But time will turn and the Flat will remain, distant and silent, salty crust unbroken, being – not even waiting, as people might, for the earth to change its mind, thrust up another range of igneous rock to knock storms down, or rip another hole to flood down another five hundred feet of water.

Nevada is an affair of the mind, overpowering in its unbroken vistas, remarkable in its absence of sound. It absorbs my thoughts or sets me free to think, until I begin to feel like a limb of wood petrifying, each cell slowly being replaced. Forget regret. Forget the unrequited toil. Forget the dreams fading in the light that just now licks Fox Mountain with a blush of rose. That is the lesson of the Flat.

Mom and Pa got a pretty choice place on the Flat,
right on Tuledad Creek.

I s'pose I could start with some of the first things I
remember, I s'pose, when I was growin' up. Mom and
Pa didn't meet till they got here in the country. Pa's name
was Burney Langston. Her name was Pearl Davidson. Pa
was born in Ar-kansas. His folks moved to California,
down in that Fresno country. They started up a prune
orchard and grapes for raisins. After Pa's mother died, his
Pa took up an advertisement for a new wife. He had all
those kids and I guess he needed some help, but he got
more than he figured on. Aunt Ada told Jessie and me, "Pa
said he saw Hell when she stepped off the train. We could
do nothing to please her." When Pa was eight years old, he
tripped over his shoelace or somethin' and dumped a whole
bucket of milk on the kitchen floor. I guess that new step-
mother lost her head. She took after him with the hand ax.
Aunt Ada said Pa busted out the screen door like a scared
rabbit and she was in a full gallop right behind with that
hatchet. Pa made it to the neighbor place and ran smack
into a man who was visiting over there. That was Lige
Richardson. Well, when Grandpa come home that night
Lige Richardson went over to see him. He said if he could

take Pa to his ranch in Surprise he would raise him and make sure he went to school. Grandpa let him go.

Mom lived in Louisiana but she was born in I-o-way. I remember hearin' her say that. She told us kids her folks had a farm. Her dad died when she was just a girl. He'd stopped plowing to talk to some guy come along the road and got chilled. He died of pneumonia. There were no hired hands to finish the plowing so Mom and her three sisters took turns behind the ox hangin' onto the plow. She called it a belly buster. Then the ox took sick and went down. The sisters took turns sitting by him, brushing flies from his face with a hank of grass or switch of leaves. Mom said they sang hymns to see him safe to Heaven.

I don't know if they lost the place or what but she come West. She hired out when she got here. She was the private housekeeper on the Dunn Ranch down on the Smoke Creek. Then she moved to the Moultin Ranch, that's the Dodge Ranch now, over on the Madeline. The other reason she left home was one of her cousins started in courtin' her and her family sent her out to stay with her sister, Kate. Aunt Kate come out to visit some relatives a few years earlier and married Frank Gooch. He told somebody he wanted to marry Kate 'cause when she finished sweepin' the floor, she hung the broom upside-down to keep the bristles from wearin' out. I guess he figured she'd be careful with his money that

*Ma and Pa got married
and filed on our place on Duck Flat.*

way. Mom quit the job at the Moultin Ranch. The kid was spoiled rotten and the folks wanted her to wait on him like they did so she quit and caught a ride over to Surprise with Lige Richardson. That's how she come to keep house for him. He had a stage stop a few miles east of the Bare Ranch. The west fence line of the Richardson Place was on the California border. It was a big two-story house, five big rooms downstairs and four bedrooms on the second floor. He mainly took in freighters and people ridin' the mail stage. Those freighters cut off hard miles from the Madeline Plains by going over the top to Tuledad Canyon and comin' into Surprise from the south. From there it was an easy day to Eagleville. I don't know how long Mom and Pa worked for Lige Richardson before they got married but Mom said that he got sick and wanted to go back to his family in the east. They took him to Reno and put him on the train, then they got married and filed on our place on Duck Flat.

In 1928 Lige found a book in an abandoned house listing eighty-five registered voters. Like so much of Nevada, the Flat is littered with the tailings of optimistic homesteaders. Fence lines, surveyed by the length of a man's stride, the sight of his eye, and the depth of his character, still wander the landscape.

The curiosity is that anyone stood before a ledger listing township and range descriptions, matched one up with a wave on a surveyor's map, and chose Duck Flat for life. The Homestead Act of 1863 was little more than a political plan for the settlement of vast undesirable acres of the West. Anyone willing to sign the contract received deeds to 160 acres of public land after it was cleared, improved, and lived on for five years. To a man, single or with a family, it was an opportunity for a start, for a chance to own a little land. The cost? Five years' hard work and an ideal. The homesteaders sang:

> *I've got 160 acres full of sunshine.*
> *I've got 160 acres of the best.*
> *Got an old stove there that'll cook three square*
> *And a bunk where I can lay me down to rest.*
>
> *Up at dawn to greet the sun*
> *I've forgotten what a care or worry means.*
> *Head for home when day is done*
> *With my pocket money jingling in my jeans.*

I've got 160 acres in the valley.
I've got 160 million stars above.
Got an old paint hoss, I'm the guy who's boss
On the 160 acres that I love.

Burney Langston and Pearl Davidson were two of those homesteaders. Their first child, born in the fall of 1908, was named Henry Elijah Langston in honor of their dearest friend. Nearly eighty years later he leaned against the pole fence beside me.

I know Mom was lonely on the Flat. She said she wouldn't see another woman for six months. Before I was born she used to saddle up a horse, put Lige up in front of her and ride over Tuledad Mountain to visit Mrs. Marr for a few days. She did that until Mrs. Marr died in childbirth with Harry.

Jessie

Four of us were born on the Flat. Jessie's next to me and she's almost three years younger. Then Don and Jack. Margaret and Pearl were born in Reno. We left the Flat when I was about eight years old. See, my birthday is in August so I didn't go to school until I was nine. They had a school way over there by the old Salt Lake Place, but it was a long ways to the thing in the winter. The folks decided to move into Reno to get us kids in school. We went to the Mary S. Dotten School and they had good teachers. My first teacher was Miss Barber and gee, she was swell. The second was Miss Shade, a tall, slim gal. Then Miss Powers, Miss Smith. I can't remember my fifth grade teacher. They changed in the middle of the year and I just can't remember. Miss Harrison was next, then Miss Radley, Miss Prowly, and Miss Lauger.

The Claim Is Set

Lige tried to live an ordinary life but he was born to the Flat and it marks its own. Not all, but some. He went to Reno's school when he turned nine, stared at plain wood walls, and dreamed.

His mother knew he needed what other children learned in school. She thought he needed more than the Flat could give: more than horses fat and fleshy, more than working with his father hiring out in haying time, more than shoveling gravel in the cart, driving Chappo stop and go, filling chuckholes in the road. Burney turned his horses loose. He watched them trotting first, then buck and run, and rear around in play, the mare nipping Chappo's neck, until they drank and crossed the creek and fed away.

Lige tried to live an ordinary life and waited for summer's smell on the Flat where Uncle Dave held the fort alone. They hayed their fields and Uncle Dave's beside, helped Mike White, hired out at Mando Camp, and ran their horses in off Tuledad and Cottonwood Mountain, and the Coppersmiths, if they strayed.

Burney carved a goose for Pearl the Christmas before they married. He laid it on her palm. She didn't look. Her fingers loved it first. With the stub blade of his pocketknife he had planed the long neck smooth, crosshatched the wings folded close to its body. The goose was not carved in flight moving forward to another season but grounded, head extended in a posture she knew was courtship, and when it came up from his back the feathers took the air of love.

Pearl placed it on the sill where she could see it as she did her work. Sunlight passed over its back from morning to the end of day, sliding down the thin legs to spread feet flattened, holding down. Sturdy as Burney was. Strong.

One day the goose was gone from the sill. Pearl remembered a woman on the noon stage whose eyes locked on it. She had gotten up from the table, her reaching hand fell furtive when Pearl turned. But she must have slipped it from the window while Pearl filled the table pitcher at the pump.

Pearl didn't tell Burney for several days. He took a hard line on dishonesty and she wanted no trouble for him. She placed a short vase of lupine and sage on the sill to distract her eye from wanting her courting goose.

Lige was Burney's second gift, long limbed, cleanly carved. On Saturday mornings when she crumbed the week's bread scraps into a bowl of milk and set the children on the stoop, each with a spoon, so she could mop the floors, Lige treated Jessie's portion fair. He was Burney's shadow. He understood the world around him. But he was growing weedy. He needed fresh ideas. He needed other children and school. She loved Burney all the more when he agreed to move from the Flat to Reno for winter. In the fall he packed them off for town.

For a year or two the family came back in June, but then babies kept Pearl near the doctor. Burney and Lige returned alone to work the horses. When summer pushed toward September, leaving – figured in and spoken of – was easier and harder each time. Lige missed his mom and the kids but he was suited for the Flat.

In the summer of Lige's fourteenth year Burney took him to gather horses and boyhood fell away. He was in camp as one of the men. He tried to think as they did, do as they did, be where they wanted him to be, stay until they released him. He rode fast behind the horses, raced beside their slick, round backs, over rocks and brush, swales and ravines, felt earth give way then rise like a wall. His heart hammered in his ears. Fear was an iron spoon in his mouth.

Lige remembered each horse gathered – color, age, markings, home range, where it would go if it got away. He saw how the men cared for their saddle horses and did the same. The horse was his legs, his servant, his friend. He held the manatha all day long until his horses' keen ears showed him a rider coming. Someday it would be him.

There were lots of range horses in those days 'cause everybody handled 'em then, you know, just like people do cattle now, 'cause that was what a lot of 'em was makin' a livin' at. Old Tom Marr was out there, my dad, that Salt Lake outfit, there was seven of those guys. Everybody had a few. Some of those old horses were still runnin' in the country when I come back out here in '28. Horses was all they had to use in those days. They hayed with 'em, farmed, all kinds of workhorses, buggy horses, and the cavalry bought a lot of horses. Anything they had to do they used horses. They just run out on the range, everybody, all of 'em, rodeared in the spring of the year, brand the colts, cut studs. They hand-bred their mares so they'd herd 'em, see. Pa did that. Jim Marr herded horses for his uncle, Tom Marr. I heard Jim tell about it. He said then if you wanted to get under a tree an' sit down in the shade you had to look to find a juniper, and now, the darned things are takin' the country. They're thick everywhere.

Anyway, you had to herd your mares in the daytime, take 'em out so they could eat. Then they'd check 'em every morning with their stud horse or whatever they used for a teaser. My dad had a Jack and a big white Percheron horse he called Sunday. I don't know how many mules he raised, but some.

My dad was a pretty good hand with workhorses. Boy, if anybody could get any pull out of 'em, he could. I don't know what he did to 'em but them buggers'd get down and scratch. Some guys talk to their team all the time, encouragin' 'em, you might say. One thing he always said about workhorses is, if you're drivin' a team, why, just keep your mouth shut, then when you speak to them they know that it's time to do somethin'. When we left here to go down below we were goin' out from the Evans place and the road went up and then cut back along the hill. It was muddy and not an extra good road either so he had six horses on. I just happened to be watchin' when he started along that grade. I thought they was goin' pretty good but he just spoke to 'em and by golly, you could just see every horse put a little more pep into it.

In 1923, the summer I came out to Duck Lake to stay with my dad, him and the Marr boys, Jim, Harry, and Brin, got together and decided to go to the Buffalo Hills to run horses for a few days. Just gather a little bunch. So we camped at Rye Patch. The next morning we saddled up and left camp early. As we went along we'd gather up a little bunch of horses. Range horses were used to bein' handled in those days.

We'd just pick 'em up and drive 'em as we went along. Just collected them and pretty soon we'd have a bunch, thirty or forty head of horses, maybe as many as a hundred. That was the manatha.

Down in the Buffalo Hills we had a certain place where we held the manatha. There are three buttes stuck up in the air, and out in between these buttes is a big flat with junipers most all the way around the outside of it. Just happens to be the way it's laid out. Trails come up through there from every direction.

My dad and Jim had run horses down there and knew what horses in that country would do. They said you could start a bunch of horses anywhere in the Buffaloes, and it's pretty big country, but if you followed 'em long enough, they'd go through that flat. If you had the manatha there and could get 'em stopped, well, that's how we caught 'em.

They were wild buggers down in that country. Studs, some of 'em three or four years old, and mares, same way, all unbranded. Never been handled. You'd know 'cause if they'd been handled all the colts would've been branded when they was suckin' their mothers. So when you get an unbranded three-year-old, you know he's never been in a corral before and not used to bein' handled. After you get 'em in the manatha, they get used to seein' a man ahorse-back, but you have to be careful with 'em.

The Buffalo Hills is in that country south of the Flat. Like you was goin' on the road to Gerlach and when you get over there by Round Mountain, why, there's a road takes off to the right. You follow that road and it was ten miles from Mike White's place to Stone Corrals, a spring with a rock stockade corral where we used to hold the manatha at night.

Anyway, we was ridin' at Stone Corral and we'd been runnin' long enough so we had a good manatha, quite a little bunch of horses. We went right up the creek, up past Stone Corrals and up to the head of the water. The Marr boys knew where they wanted to hold the manatha, right on top of the ridge, up where you could see around. They left me and Bruce Marr with the manatha that day and all we had to do was keep 'em in a bunch and be on the lookout for somebody comin' in with a bunch. Harry and Jim and Brin and Pa went out lookin' for some horses.

Jim showed up first with a bunch of wild browns. When they hit that manatha they was runnin' their best. We stopped 'em but he was right alongside of 'em. That was the good part. You wonder how he could be there, but he was there. He had his hat in his hand, standin' in his stirrups, they were all runnin' their level best.

Just as soon as they got mixed up in the other horses they stopped. We held 'em for a couple of hours but they worked around, got together again in the manatha, and by gosh, they broke out and we lost 'em all. They didn't stick around, them buggers. They were that wild. They left. They just about ran over me doin' it.

The thing that's hard to understand was how Jim could be with 'em when they hit the manatha, but he was there, right alongside of 'em. That was the kind of horse runner he was. A fella has to be about half horse himself to outsmart them buggers.

Where the road goes east out of Surprise Valley the travel-er faces a signpost at the state line. It doesn't say, Welcome to Nevada. It says, NEVADA.

A compact car filled to the window sash with passengers stopped next to me and my husband, John, riding at the tail end of six hundred dry cows. It was April 1974 and we were with a handful of buckaroos trailing our cattle to summer pasture in northwestern Nevada. A spring squall had been blowing since dawn and we hunched into our slickers. We might have looked dangerous but actually we were harmless and cold. The driver of the little Honda unrolled his window a crack and, aiming his question upward as if to the surface of water, said, "We're trying to get home. Will this road take us to Pennsylvania?"

"Eventually," John replied.

It was only a guess on his part, of course. He didn't know what "home" meant to the misplaced traveler.

As you leave Cedarville going east on 299 a Cal-Trans sign warns, NO SERVICES 100 MILES. Not only no services but no people, except for a few sturdy folks who ranch in the space of the Great Basin. Unlike the Pennsylvanians, I'm not anxious alone in the desert the way I am where freeways merge and cars rush in their lanes. Fellow travelers speed unaware of me though we are nearly shoulder to shoulder, their eyes glancing off mine. I imagine us as particles flying past each other into a void. Cities fill me with a deep sense of isolation. I am at odds with what others accept as normal. I find security in the open-ness of land, the opportunity of the bare earth. It is not so much what I fear but what I need. The people in the Honda were pos-sibly as far as they could imagine from their home and I was at the center of mine.

My father and his brothers ran wild horses in the rimrock coun-try along the John Day River in eastern Oregon and swam in its pools with Warm Springs Indian kids. They trailed cattle to Hep-pner, Madras, or The Dalles, and broke horses for neighboring ranchers. Dad won Mom's heart riding broncs in the rodeo. The two of them spent their lives raising and training horses so I came by my love of horses honestly. For as long as I could remember the soft-whiskered muzzle of the horse has blown the sweet scent of grass or wind or the pleasures of freedom into my hair. I could see ahead better from their withers than from my own feet. I stored up Dad's singing "The Strawberry Roan" and him trading a horse for a pair of beaded buckskin gloves to be reeled out in daydreams. As I rode in the woods back of the house, Dad's stories galloped alongside with details cowboy movie stars left out, the very details I needed for a whole picture of life in the West.

The first of October 1970 John Hussa telephoned an invitation to help gather the Hussa Ranch cattle from the Sheldon Ante-lope Refuge, sixty miles northeast of their home ranch in Sur-prise Valley. If I had been on a horse when I heard his voice I might have been able to see what was ahead for me, but there I stood, flat-footed on the adobe soil. Something smarter than me said yes. I left the San Francisco Bay area before dawn and by sunset I was four hundred miles away in the cab of a '56 International stock truck, John at the wheel, crossing the state line into Nevada.

On that dirt road into the desert I felt a stirring sense of something familiar that existed just beyond the balance of my disillusion. In the headlights jackrabbits darted willy-nilly, reminding me of my own progress over the past few years. The black of the desert night leaned its total power against the windows of the truck, holding me off until morning, but my eyes couldn't have gathered in the feeling that seeped like alkali dust through the floorboards. It wasn't one turning draw wrapping shadows under a distant rim. It wasn't one silent moment holding the pinpoint that was me. John's face glowed in the dashlight. He talked easily about Badger Camp and the other permitees I would be meeting. The truck swayed and lumbered with the weight of saddle horses, head to tail in the back. I listened to the man, so steady, so sure.

The lanterns were out in the cabin at Badger camp but I could smell the smoke of the bunkroom fire. John carried my bedroll to a camp trailer uphill from the spring. He took the world away with him in the narrow beam of his flashlight.

I'd hardly closed my eyes when Bill Heryford bellowed from the cabin porch, "Get up, you lazy bastards!" It was a command I took to heart.

My clothes had the soft folds of my everyday; what I didn't know was outside in the dark. The trailer door swung open to a sky roan with stars. Constellations were familiar brands on the night's hide. Yet nearer. Brighter. I dashed icy water on my face from the spring, felt the crunch of frozen grass under my feet, and wondered if the gathering of people inside the cabin, their noise, their movement was pocketed by the desert's cold breath as a splinter is surrounded by a body's work to isolate an intrusion. My wet hand froze on the doorknob until I warmed it to my turning.

Jane and Charles Stevens pampered us with food that made good manners difficult. She fired our days with biscuits, pies, and cakes from the Home Comfort stove.

Frank Moyles was the soft-spoken one who looked into the distance and saw a cow – still as stone, or a stone that dipped a shadow as a cow would graze, and was proven right with steady binoculars, saving wasted miles.

Louie Vermillion was known for lying down in the road before a hunter's rig and when it screeched to a stop, doors flew open, hunters piled out prepared for broken bones, he would raise up on one elbow and beg a beer.

Bill, the cow boss, rode all the nasty horses that came his way and wore their scars. His father, Lee Heryford, and John's grandfather, "Hussy," had been lifelong friends and partners with P. B. Harris in the Alkali Cattle Company, a.k.a. the Badly Scattered Cattle Company. Bill's direction was fair. Men rode for him because he could and would do all of it better, longer, harder, and more – with less.

Morning opened in a light of such clarity that Blowout Mountain leaped across seven miles. I felt I could wipe green lichen under the jagged rim loose with a finger. I felt roughened to the space, feet on new soil. The smell of the country went in my lungs and stayed. Sage. Mahogany smoke. Bitterbrush. Horse sweat. The last of summer twisted in frost.

While the shippers – John's father, Walter, Bill's brother, Mark, and Charles – worked on the separating pens, the circle boys (amended "circle *crew*" to include me) loaded our horses and hauled south to Ten Mile Mountain. Bill, Frank, and Louis rode the breaks off to the west. John and I went east. We were to meet on Alkali Lake. On a ridge above a spring named for Billy McCluskey I saw my first wild horses through a thicket of the sun's glare on mahogany leaves. I thought the movement was mule deer, but my tall brown horse, Dandy, knew the shadows of horses. I only meant to get Dandy where I could have a look at the little band of sorrels and bays, but we flew together off the rim, wild horses and tame. I would have let deer go, or a coyote, and watched them trot into their own solitude, but I rode after the horses. Dandy carried me down the steep sidehill, across the wash, in lunges up the other side. Rocks, brush, drops, holes were good footing to him – dog after the rabbit, hawk hunting the long grass – he ran beside them an easy mile. I pressed the horses around the flat toward the Potholes, where I figured John would be. I pulled Dandy up and let them go. It was the desert's first kiss.

I couldn't explain to John why I'd chased the horses. He smiled. "It's something a person's just gotta do, forget the dangers, and own those horses for a few strides."

We married the next Christmas Eve and I became Mom to John's six-year-old daughter, Katie. Our life in Surprise Valley was simple, seasonal: winter feeding of livestock, spring branding and turnout. Once the cattle were on the desert and out of the way for the summer feed season we dragged meadows, harrowed, drilled oats, and tended irrigation water that would dwindle come June when the mountain streams dried up. John's mother, Kay, canned, pickled, dried, or froze as the garden and orchard ripened, beginning with cherries straight through to fall's green tomatoes on her sunny windowsills. An earthy smell hugged potatoes, onions, winter squash, carrots in the cool cellar. Nothing went to waste. Thinned carrots were peeled, spiced, and packed in jars. Bricks of butter lined the freezer. She served meat and hot bread at every meal – six, noon straight up, and six. At lunch and dinner she served two kinds of vegetables, meat, salad, potatoes, gravy, hot bread, and dessert. We ate like field hands. We *were* field hands.

Every year in June we celebrated John's birthday at the Alkali Cattle Company's Wall Canyon camp. Feed in the desert's low country was done. We gathered, branded the calves born since turnout, and pushed them up to summer country on Badger Mountain. We cut alfalfa as soon as we got home and in between cuttings, sharpened the sickles, and laid the wild hay down. Haying continued until school took up. We took summer outings in the mountains between hay crops for winter wood and in August picked chokecherries, elderberries, and wild plums.

In the fall we went to Badger to ride all the country again, gather the cattle into the field, separate out loads for each ranch, and ship them home. The fall gather lasted ten days to two weeks with a reride after the first big snow. Cow work continued at home until the big calves were weaned, the new calves branded up, pairs in one bunch, drys in another. We began feeding hay about Christmastime and calved heifers in the spring.

Our family entertainment centered around ball games, dances, barbeques, and rodeos in nearby towns. Hard work and lack of variety fired our imaginations and secured a kind of satisfaction in my life. It was a rhythm Dad and Mom had lost track of, but one that worked for me. I moved away from houses built on the pleasant rolling hills of California thick as the wild oats that once grew there and reached past their dreams of a different security to find contentment in work on the land within our own fences, in a community made up of neighbors whose lives were in step with ours, bound by seasons that move in their own life cycle.

I try to see the desert through the stranger's eyes. A dirt road. One hundred miles. The longest straight stretch, maybe ten miles across Long Valley, is like knocking an arrow aimed at Paint Mountain. The road passes beside the knob of banded sandstone punched up from the inland seabed. Otherwise, it looks empty. No sign of the early 1900s homesteads that dotted it like pepper on an egg. The stories are the human parts we must remember – the play, poetry, music, the art of the cold desert. What else gives it definition? What else connects its depth to us? A band of riders behind a herd of cows was the only sign of life encountered by the people in the car. Now those travelers are a part of the story left behind.

Sometime in the late 1920s a camp tender left Surprise with supplies for a sheepherder. His mind was content on other things until he reached the place where the sheep should have been scattered out, feeding as they moved south. He went on, his eyes searching for the slow-moving smear of sheep, dogs, mule, man. Never meeting them. Past the place they were to bed the night before. Further on. He worried, coyotes, cats, lost Spanish herder. What could take a band of sheep so far off course? He went over their conversation the week before when he hefted the pack up on the mule, tossed the rope across, pointed to a blue gray peak, counted out seven fingers. He remembered clearly, the boy had nodded.

He drove the truck down every side track east and west, turning back, pressing on, until the day was nearly gone. Then there was a rising hill and on its bland face bedded in the round like a full moon settling for a night's repair, he found the band.

To find the lost, relief contends with anger: which spreads down the arms and which shows on the face is left to chance. The boy's expression was part contrite, part mischief, part delight as he explained. A passing buckaroo told him of a dance, and a schoolmarm – brand new and pretty, it was said. The herder spoke in Spanish but his hands said, "The sheep, I take the sheep the way your horse's tail is pointing."

"Well," the buckaroo replied, "Go that way if you must, but I learned early it's best when riding a horse to follow the head." He scooped his arm to round up the grazing herd and laughed, "Bring the sheep along."

That piece of sagebrush country stands up different now from the rest and we tell time and time again – if only to ourselves – the story of a Spanish herder who took his sheep to Vya for the dance.

The desert gathers in travelers of many kinds. Some stray into it, others push across with purpose, denying or not recognizing the power, the unanswered questions, the nick of humor that rests until it's rubbed open.

On a near-zero day in January 1978 Sophie and Lynn drove

their "tomato can," a faded red '53 Ford panel wagon, on the shortcut from 395 to the Smoke Creek Desert. They were surrounded by sacks of potatoes piled around their feet near the heater to keep them freezing. At Sand Pass, the crossroads to Flannigan, Wendel, and the Never Sweat Hills, they came on a pair of hitchhikers. On a normal summer day the back road around the Smoke Creek Desert is not a likely place to catch a ride. In the winter the possibility would be considerably less. He was a brokendown buckaroo, beat-up saddle dumped next to him in six inches of fresh snow. She was in full makeup, eyelashes pasted on, hair poofed and pinned, dressed in slippers and what looked to be a bathrobe, stomach oblonged in the final month of pregnancy. Lynn stopped, slid the door aside. The buckaroo asked if they could get a lift to Deep Hole, a ranch nearly thirty miles away. He threw his saddle in the back, helped the woman in, and climbed in beside her. Except for the gurgle of a hip flask, they sat quietly on the floor. They offered no explanation of a stalled truck or out of gas. At Deep Hole the couple got out. He opened the gate for her, then slung the saddle over his shoulder and they walked toward the old house, hand in hand. The buckaroo and his showgirl.

But make no mistake, the desert must be respected. Wide open vistas that are a treatment for the soul can be too far to safety.

Years back a buckaroo rode away from camp. No one could know what happened, but the search party guessed that his horse bucked him off. They found the ashes of three signal fires before they came to his body. One leg was badly shattered. Ravens had gotten his eyes. The boy who cooked and tended camp saw his horse standing outside the corral the first day. He could have ridden to headquarters for help but instead he unsaddled the horse, let him into the field, and said nothing. Bad blood between them turned the boy's mind hard against the buckaroo and he used the desert as his weapon.

As late as the 1990s, a young couple with their baby disregarded the power of the desert in winter when they attempted to cross that same country in a pickup. For nearly a week they floundered in the snow, stuck, unstuck, stuck again. Finally they abandoned their rig and took shelter in a blowhole in Hell Creek Canyon. They had been without food for days. Her milk had dried up so she melted snow in her mouth and dribbled the warmed water into her baby son's mouth. Snow was their worst enemy and their only sustenance. The husband left them in the shallow shelter to try to reach help. Exhausted, with frozen feet, he was seen by the road crew superintendent on the edge of Long Valley. Two of his men joined him and followed the husband's directions across forty miles of snowbound desert. Incredibly they reached her just before dark, before another storm that would have swallowed her and her baby into its callus of cold. In the pickup one of the men, Dusty Ferguson, remembered his lunch pail was in the tool box in the back. But as he opened the black pail, he drew it back from her saying, "Oh, gosh. Maybe you should wait until you see the doctor."

"Give me the orange," she said firmly. It rolled from his hand into the cup of her palm. Her other hand closed it in. When she broke it open a little rain of oily citron juice filled the pickup cab. The scent was remarkable. The baby's eyes locked on the orange. She peeled a section away and put the tip into his mouth. His tiny fingers clutched around hers. He sucked it as a nipple.

I've often had it pointed out that I am slow at catching on, always was, so it's not surprising I stumbled through thirty years before I found the seed of my life. And then it rolled across my palm leaving me to wonder at its significance, with no expectation of a second seed to suggest a direction. John's phone call was the first seed. The desert possessed the second. I remembered the sign, no services, and slowly caught on. No help – but help yourself. I rode into it a-horseback and I'll always be thankful for that entry. Badger Mountain was beneath an inland sea in another time. A fourteen-foot fossilized fish is etched in stone off to the south. A petrified forest on the northern breaks, fallen like slash behind a crosscut saw, was standing when the bear dog, half-ton hunter, roamed in the Miocene. I've held its white-as-ivory tooth, its curve long as my middle finger. John showed me these things. He is the sower of seeds.

I hope the family found Pennsylvania again. It was their searching in an incongruous place that made me begin thinking about my own. I have abandoned the woods of the Northwest and tucked away the golden hills of northern California that were mine in school days. A look back has a filmy feel of another life, maybe even someone else's life. In the open of the desert wind carries scents and sounds to me and adds mine on. It changes moment to moment. With my back to the Warner Mountains my mind has better than two hundred miles to the east, two hundred miles to the south, two hundred miles to the north, free to roam. The few ranches or settlements are part of the landscape because they, too, belong here. I explore this inland seabed, searching across great distances to the place where the earth arches and to the bone pebbles stacked at my feet by ants on grains of sand finer yet. It is the middle ground that lulls adventure away and blends bright colors of the palette to a muddy blur. To find focus I must look fully on the extremes and ride a balance between them. Defenseless against its bitterness, sting, thorn, poison, old as granite, precious as water, abundant as sage, I am here. The nighthawk cries. I walk each swell of sand, each hollow, and because of that woman and her child, the fragrance that surrounds me is often orange.

My Pa was a pretty good hand with workhorses.

His Pa's back moved in the rhythm of toil. On the workbench the pocketknife the boy borrowed from his father, stepped on by the pan-footed Chappo, bone handle splintered, spinning on the rivet's brass pin. Lige leaned around his Pa's shoulder to see the vise grip a spike's antler, first wracking of challenge, waxy light and dark plug of growth rubbed lustrous under velvet bark.

Steady, measured, shoulder, arm, saw in a clean straight line to make the plate. Chest pressed on the drill's wooden pommel. Bright curlicues winding up the bit stem. Filed, dressed, seated on the pegs, he burred the brads to hold.

The weight – right. The feel – right. He opened the blade. Closed the blade. Laid it on Lige's palm.

Good as new, Pa. Better.

Dad was a gentle person for a man. Oh, he kept us in line, especially the boys. He never hit me but he'd whop the boys if they needed it. I don't remember a thing about Dad that was unkind and he was really good to Mom.

When we lived in Reno he came in from doin' the morning chores and he told Mom the chicken house door was open and all the hens were gone. He'd found them in the neighbor lady's chicken house. "Did you get 'em back?" Mom asked. "Well, yes," he said, "but I had to pay her for 'em." "But they're our hens," she said. "I know," Pa said, "but she's a poor old lady."

Jessie

I bummed a ride with Lawrence and Ralph's father, George Parman. He had a 1920 Dodge sedan, one where the top folds back. Lawrence told me once that George would ask his wife if it was such and such an hour and he wanted to be in Reno at such and such a time, then how fast would he have to drive to get there? She'd figure it out and say thirty-five miles an hour and that's how fast he drove, even if it was over a rock pile. Once he threw Ralph out and broke his arm.

Part 2

. . . first when he wakes up, forgets his
rider and begins to notice other things
about him; . . .

I climbed out of Parman's Dodge Sedan in Reno and started to school, but I didn't go a month. We got a report card at the end of every month and I didn't get my first report card. I know, I'd just had my birthday and that's August 10. I turned fifteen. Pa wrote in and wanted me to come out and help gather our horses, so I never did go back to school. I should have graduated out of the eighth grade the year before but I played hooky, horsed around, and didn't get passed. Didn't have anybody to blame but myself. So the next year I was going to make it all up, but it didn't work out that way.

Pa had this idea to gather some of our horses to sell. He was feelin' sick, too sick to ride a horse, but 'course I didn't know it then. He hired an Indian fella named Willy Sam to help me. Willy knew all the country and the horses and everything. Mom and Pa liked Willy. When he stayed with us he'd sleep with me. So him and I, we gathered them horses. When we got 'em to the corral, Pa separated out the ones he wanted to keep and we shipped rest. There was one black, bald-faced horse we didn't get. We had a bay horse that was a full brother to him, but I never did find that bugger that fall. I just didn't know how to ride or where to look, for sure. I was ridin' alone and went back in the country where he stayed, but now I know that I just didn't look in the right place.

'Course in the fall of the year those horses move from where they have a habit of runnin'. I think he went off down into that country toward Burnt Lake. I didn't get down in there far enough. He was still here when I come back in '28 with Dad Hicks. He was a big, snaky bugger and he didn't know the word quit when it came to pullin'.

Willy Sam and I put those horses Pa wanted to sell on the railroad at Gerlach. Up around thirty ordinary horses could fit in a car, but I'm kinda guessin'. We loaded two cars. We had most of the horses gathered, all but this black horse, and Dad wanted him, so Willy went home and I kept riding for another week or so. While I was doin' that Pa was gettin' ready to go down to California. I don't know what he had in mind exactly, I didn't ask him. All I knew was that he wanted to take this bunch of horses and all his shop and go down to that country he came from, where Uncle Dave and his sisters lived.

He finally decided to forget the black horse. He said we was flirtin' with the weather. The storms were startin' to blow in. One day it'd be nice and warm and the next a cold wind'd be blowin' up your shirttail.

We had two wagons, trailed one behind the other one. Pa drove four horses if the weather wasn't bad or if it wasn't tough pullin'. But if it was tough, he put on six. It was my job to drive the extra team and saddle horses. I had two horses that I rode, a sorrel and a bay. After I got the horses trained to follow the wagons, why, they wasn't any trouble. I just had to ride along with 'em. After we got down a ways I would go ahead of Pa and find a place to stay all night. By the time Pa got there with the wagons I'd have it all set and he could just drive right in.

We started out in the fall, before the weather got bad. We left Duck Lake and went up through Tuledad toward the Madeline. We stopped the first night at the Marrs'. We stayed around there most of the day, chewin' the rag with the Marr boys. Pa didn't seem to be in any hurry to go once he got to their place. But in the afternoon we hooked up and went on to the Evans Place, just over the hill.

The third night we stayed at the Dodge Ranch. The Anderson Brothers was livin' there then. There was two of them, big tall rawboned guys. One thing I remember about them, they had two houses about a mile or more apart. One lived in each one but they both boarded at the one further north. We slept at the south place and the next morning we had to walk down the road to the other one where we left the horses. We walked alongside of this big grain field. They had two big yellow dogs, like collies, but young dogs they were, full brothers, I think they said. Anyway, those dogs jumped a rabbit out in that field and it took right down the road. One dog was faster than the other and he ran behind the rabbit, while the slower one ran to the side. The rabbit would see the one on the side fallin' back and slow down a little and the one behind would get him.

We went right on across the Plains. We stopped at Termo and I went in the store and bought somethin', I don't remember what but it was in a little paper sack. I got on that little bay horse and the paper got to rattlin'. He didn't like that, I can tell you, and he ran away for a while. Of course, all the extra horses used the excuse for some excitement and took off buckin' and runnin'. Then Dad's team tried the same thing with him but with that big load they didn't go far. We finally got things under control again and it was good for a laugh.

That night we stayed at an old character's place over on the other side of the plains. He was a bachelor, a dirty old sucker and why we ever slept in his bed I'll never know, but we did. 'Cause he offered it to us, I guess.

We went on down through the country, kind of like the road goes now, to Adin, across Big Valley, McArthur, and so on. The people along the way were real nice. Sometimes we stayed a day or so to help with work or choppin' wood to pay our board. We took Thanksgiving dinner with a man and his family. They had a boy 'bout my age. He asked questions about runnin' wild horses and what it was like. I think he wanted to go with us.

When we got down to Maxwell, California, we camped there a few days. Pa mighta wrote home for more money, I don't know what, but anyway we got lousy when we stayed at that old dirty guy's place on the Madeline but we didn't know it, either one of us. I didn't have any idea what a louse was anyway, but I found one on me. I captured that little sucker and showed him to my dad. Oh, God! he said, we're lousier than pet coons. I'll go to town and get something to get rid of these things and you get plenty of water boilin'.

We scalded all our clothes, everything that we'd been usin', our bedding, everything. The druggist had give Pa somethin' called Blue Ointment. Every morning and night we'd shake out our beds and sprinkle that Blue Ointment over it, and before we went to bed at night we'd go over each other lookin' for those little louses. We was about eat up with those lousy little things.

What I hated about that was that we had stayed at some nice houses on the way down and I'm sure we had to leave some of those things behind. You can just imagine what those people would think about you, and you couldn't blame 'em either.

There wasn't anything unusual that happened until we got way down in the valley. We stayed on a big ranch that hired a lot of men and they told us about a way we could go through the country, cut off quite a bit, and miss the main highway. So we did, but a week or so before that, when we was up in the mountains we was goin' down a grade and Pa was on the outside edge of a drop-off when a carload of people came up the road, meetin' us. One of the horses that I was a-drivin' stepped out in front of them just as they was even with the leaders on the wagon. Well, they cut loose with their cockeyed horn. The team would have gone anywhere if they could have got away but the bank was solid rock straight up about thirty feet and the other side was straight down, so they just had to take it. But those horses didn't forget that car and its blamed horn.

Well, the day we left the big ranch it was rainin'. I never saw rain come down like it did in that country. Water had been runnin' alongside the road and cut a gully six or eight feet deep. We were just about even with the start of that gully when a car come along. Well, the horses remembered that other car on the mountain and their blamed horn honkin' and they jackknifed on Pa. He wasn't lookin' for that, a'course. There was room to pull behind that gully and Pa made it too, all but the last wheel on the trail wagon. It went into that ditch and pulled the whole outfit right in on top of it. We had three horses down on the bottom in that wash, three on top and two wagons on their side in there. It was rainin' cats an' dogs and what a mess!

The guys in the car didn't have anything to do with it but they stopped and helped us. We had to unhook the horses and get 'em out of the wash, then unload the wagons. Then we hooked the leaders up and they had to pull the wagons out alone. Now, you never saw anything dig and scratch mud like those leaders did, just the two of them. It took most of the day to get straightened out and loaded again. We were wet from the skin out and muddy! God! It was a mess. None of the horses were hurt but I sure felt sorry for 'em. Pa worked till I thought he was gonna drop, but we went on. No use to stop, he said. There was no way to get dried off. Couldn't even start a fire in all that rain.

It was after that that Pa started havin' these spells. He'd wake up and he couldn't get his breath, so he'd kick me out and I'd get a fire goin'. He'd sit by the fire awhile and pretty soon he'd get all right. As time went on the spells started comin' on everyday, and a little earlier everyday, too. The first ones were in the night, and pretty soon, it was daylight.

We got to Lodi and a spell came on him in the night and some people took him to the hospital in French Camp. Then I was left with the outfit alone. I didn't have any idea where to go except I knew about where he was headed, that's all. So the next morning I picked out four of those horses that I knew I could handle, the wheelers and the pointers, caught a saddle horse, tied him behind a wagon, and took down the road.

Tire Shrinker

'Course then I had to drive into a place to find out about the stayin' all night. The first place I went into was three or four miles off the road. Couldn't stay, so by the time I come out I lost quite a bit of time. It got dark and fog, man, talk about fog. It was thick. I got back out on the highway and a taxi pulled up beside me and the guy said, You better put out a light. I didn't have a light, I told him, and I asked him how far it was to Stockton.

You're on the wrong road to get to Stockton, he said. In that fog I got off on the wrong road and he said I was on the way to a country club. I had to get turned around, so I found a wide place, no fences. I got off the wagon and looked it over, and it looked all right. There was a little dip right along the road and since it had been rainin', it was soft, but in the dark I didn't notice, so I pulled around. I made the turn all right but when I pulled back on the road the front wheels went into that little ditch and I was stuck, right to the axle.

I knew I couldn't get out with the horses on that pavement. They were tired too. I had drove 'em all day. So I just pulled them over to the side of the road and unhooked the team, tied them to the wagon wheel, and fed 'em some grain. I had my bed in the wagon so I crawled into it and went to sleep. The next morning I started unloadin' that trail wagon. I didn't think I could pull it out of there with all that weight, and on the pavement, too. Well, Pa had a blacksmith shop, a big anvil, and a tire shrinker in that trail wagon. A lot of heavy stuff. I had some of it unloaded when some guys come along in a truck. They could see the predicament I was in, so they said they'd pull the wagons onto the road with their truck. They helped me load that heavy stuff back into the wagon. Some of it was too heavy and I know I couldn't have loaded it by myself. Then they pulled me back on the road. I hooked up the horses and started off again.

When I got into Stockton I ran right into one of those feed yards where you can keep a horse on board. There was an old guy runnin' it and when I told him my predicament, that I wanted to look out of there and find some pasture for the horses, he gave me a corral for my horses and threw 'em some hay. They spent time rollin' in the dirt and then they went to eatin'. It had been quite a long time since they had been let loose and weren't tied to something. The old guy let me throw my bed in the barn and shared his dinner with me. It had been a day or so since I ate last.

Good Deeds

The next morning I started ridin'. One day I'd go one way and the next day I'd go another way. One mornin' as I was goin' through town this guy crossed the street in front of me afoot. He stopped and was lookin' my horse over. He wanted to know if I wanted to sell the horse I was ridin'. God, no, I said, I need him. So I asked him if he knew where a fella could get some pasture. Yeah, he said, he had lots of pasture along the San Joaquin. Grass knee high, lots of water, a good place. So we made a deal right there on the street and he told me how to find the place. But it was too late to start that day, so I waited till the next morning.

The first thing the next morning I hooked up the four horses. The fog on the pavement made it slick and the horses weren't used to the darned pavement, too. They were desert horses. We were all like fish out of water.

One of my wheelers, this bay horse, got to pullin' extra hard, and the harder he pulled the more he slipped, and he finally fell. He got clear over the tongue on the other horse's side. There I was, and I knew I was gonna have to unhook him to get him up. About that time some guys come along in a car and wanted to know if they could be of help. I said they sure could, if they'd just stand out there in front of the leaders and hold 'em I'd get the horse up and hook him up again.

64

So I did, but when that horse fell down he broke that back band that goes around the hames to hold the hames together up on top, and I didn't notice it. So I went on and when I got right down in the main part of Stockton the breechin', it was all breechin' harness, fell down on the singletree behind him. There I was right in the middle of town with streetcars and automobiles, and those horses just weren't used to that kind of stuff. If I got down off the wagon I wouldn't have had any control over the team, so I asked this guy to pick up that breechin' and hook it over the hames, or anywhere, so I could get out of the doggone traffic and fix it. You'da thought I asked him to pet a rattlesnake, but he finally got up his nerve. The horse was all right. The guy was more scared than the horse was.

I was headed to French Camp, where Pa was in the hospital, but I was afraid to take time to go in and see him because I didn't know how long it would take me to get to Tracy. I didn't want to get caught in the dark in strange country, so I thought I should go on. When I got to French Camp there was a wide, flat place so I pulled off the highway and thought I'd check my outfit and see if everything was all right. I'd lost my darned saddle horse. He'd been tied behind the trail wagon and the chain had come unsnapped or somethin'. He was gone, anyway. Well, I needed that sucker so I drove the team over to the fence and tied 'em up and started back afoot. I figured I'd find him along the road someplace. I got a ride and went clear to Stockton and never seen a sign of that darned horse. I knew I couldn't fool around and leave that darned team so I started back and got a ride to the wagon. I got them off the highway that night. I had to go clear down to Tracy the next day, then three miles out to the ranch from town. When I went through Tracy I didn't think about leavin' my darned saddle there 'cause I was gonna have to go back to Stockton the next day to try to find that saddle horse I'd lost and get the other horses. So the next morning I had to pack my saddle clear back to Tracy where I could catch the bus.

When we got into Stockton I see some kids with my horse down off the edge of the road. I hailed the driver to a stop and went back. The snap had come unfastened and he was draggin' the halter chain. They'd tied him to a fence. I got on him with just the halter and rode to the feed yard.

The next day I started out with the horses. Of course, they was used to followin' the wagon and when I started just drivin' 'em loose, with nothing for 'em to follow, they didn't know where to go. God, they run into every gate that was open into every lousy yard. Didn't miss one, I don't believe. I give both of my saddle horses out just tryin' to keep them blamed horses gathered up. I finally got to Stockton and I tried to go around town, the main part of it, and ended up in a lousy little suburb off to the side. Green lawns, God! Did I have hell. I was ready to give the whole bunch away. I'd get 'em out of one yard and they'd run into the next and around the house, under clotheslines, through gardens and flowerbeds. People were yellin' at me to get 'em out and I was doin' my level best, but it wasn't good enough.

About then a little kid on a bicycle come along, so I got him to ride on the sidewalk – asked him if he would – to keep the horses out in the street, so they wouldn't run on those darned lawns. As soon as I had some help they lined right out and went along good. He knew all the streets, too, and showed me some shortcuts I'd never a known about, so we were out of town in no time at all. When I got in the clear he pulled up to go back and I told him I wanted to pay him for his help. Aw no, he said. Said he was a boy scout and he was supposed to do a good deed for somebody everyday. Well, I can tell you, he did his good deed that day.

Broken Glass

Well, anyway, I got the horses back on the main highway again. I'd run the heck out of 'em all day and they was give out. It got dark and the road was just a string of cars. You could see their lights one right after another for miles, not travelin' fast but lots of 'em. Those darned horses took right down the white line, down the middle of the pavement, one behind the other one in a little dog trot, and they just kept a-goin'. I couldn't keep 'em off of there, so I rode off down in the gutter and stayed behind. It was dark, holy smoke, it was dark. Two different horses got hit by cars, didn't hurt the horses but they knocked out the cars' headlights. The rest of the horses went out around the cars and right on down the road. Didn't even stop. Boy, was I glad to get off that highway, I tell you.

I got the horses turned into the field at Tracy, I don't know, it was late. I rolled up in my saddle blanket like a dog and went to sleep.

The next day the guy that owned the field give me a job, plowin' for him. I knew I was gonna need some money for Pa's doctor bills so I took it.

I got to go see Pa once. Had to just bum a ride. He didn't know me, not too good anyway. He was kinda out of his head. The nurse hadn't shaved him, God. His whiskers was long. I never saw him with whiskers. He always shaved, every morning. She wanted me to shave him. I just looked at her. I didn't say a word.

Death Came Riding

His fork smashed down against the saddle fork rising. Forgetting turns. Forgetting doors. Forgetting faces. Fifteen-year-old boy used to sagebrush and seeing into far country. Fifteen-year-old shadow along green walls. Remembering horses, the jolt when they snatched their head, the ache between his eyes, between his legs. Nothing a horse did hurt like the thing waiting down the hall.

Four hundred miles from home. Wagon, horses tied outside the city hospital filled with strangers. His father's face floating between sheets and pillow, already partly gone down dark halls. Stubble beard dark in deep creases. Safety razor, basin, soap on the nightstand. Unscrew the head, unwrap the blade, lay it in, twist it together. Pour water in the basin. Lather the hard, square soap. Laying hands on the face he had looked on with respect, loved, but had not touched since he was a baby.

Stiff skin, whiskers rough against his palms. Cool stiff skin. Soap bubbles bleeding out on the pillow. Razor scraping a clean, smooth swath down the gaunt tarnished face of his father, who died before the shave was finished.

Mom came down. I was sure glad to see her.

That place in Tracy where Lige was workin' was a terrible set-up. Mom said the cook shack was filthy and the food wasn't fit to eat. The stew had whole carrots and potatoes and it didn't taste like anything she had ever eaten before. She said the guy had really taken advantage of Lige. He offered 'em so much for Pa's whole outfit, wagons, shop, horses, the works. Lige was just a kid, he didn't know the value of things. They both knew it wasn't enough but Mom needed to get back home. I was takin' care of the kids and, you know, the girls were real young. Margaret four and little Pearl wasn't even two yet and both sick. Later we found out it was polio. The guy just cheated them. It's as simple as that.

Jessie

There were two washin' machines waitin' on the back porch in the snow. The kids said a man delivered 'em for Mom to try. An Easywash and a Maytag.

It was a good deal. Ten dollars a month to pay the thing off. We decided on the Maytag. I told Mom, we'll take in laundry. I'll help, do anything Pa did. I'll do anything.

Pa's family said they'd pay all the expenses if Mom let Pa be buried in Stockton. She didn't have any money so she agreed. What was the point, anyway, to takin' his body to Reno? It was what his family wanted. She thought it was the right thing to do. We rode the train back to Reno.

So that's what we did. Took in laundry. Then I got jobs takin' care of people's furnaces, buildin' their fires, packin' wood in, and cleanin' ashes out. Just odd jobs. We was kind of well acquainted around Reno and a lot of people was sure good to help. If a job turned up, why, they'd let us know.

Jessie quit school, too, and got a job runnin' an elevator in a building downtown. Don got a job in the stockroom at J. C. Penney's. I worked for a delivery service takin' packages all over town on a bike and telegrams for Western Union. I pruned trees, scrubbed floors, did housework, anything, I didn't care, any darned thing I could make a nickel at. So we just kept goin' along, by gosh.

Lige turned back toward the Flat and his long fingers combed several strands of horsehair caught on the fence. He began to braid them in a rhythm that eased his thinking. Black over sorrel, gray over black, sorrel over gray, over black again.

Telling the story flattened his gaze as the swing of the windmill followed the breeze east out of Express Canyon. The screen door of the house lifted and slammed and Lige looked beyond the big willow, squinting into the sun, as if he expected to see someone standing on the stoop.

Down the meadow a jackrabbit hopped into the open and stopped. The dark disk of his eye turned toward us. It touched its front feet where the overflow pipe ran and leaned forward to drink.

Black over sorrel, gray over black, sorrel over gray, over black again.

*When we first moved to Reno we didn't know anybody,
and so the first Sunday Mom scrubbed the four of us up
and took us into the Methodist church. She was baptized
Methodist but she hadn't been to a real church in years.
Well, she took us three weeks in a row and nobody spoke
to her. Nothing. It's true we didn't have new clothes but
we were clean, I tell you, Mom saw to that. She was
heartbroken. It went against everything she'd been
telling us about church. She heard the Salvation Army
playin' down on the street outside the Overland Hotel
where we were stayin'. You know, the man who formed
the Salvation Army was a Methodist. He said, You're
only preachin' to the well-to-do. What about the guys
livin' in the slums? Mom worked for the Salvation Army
from then on. I was too young to know then but Mom
used to visit the women down in the Bull Pen. She took
them flowers from our garden and talked with them.
Later, after I was married, she told me that those women
needed to know they weren't looked down on. Not by
everybody, anyway.*

Jessie

75

Mom raised ducks to sell. She penned 'em up at night and every morning we'd let 'em out on the Orr Ditch. They'd swim off and we wouldn't see 'em till evening. When the ducklings got big enough Jessie and I would take 'em down to Chinatown on Lake Street. The old men would come out of the shops and take a duckling from the wooden cage we had strapped to Jessie's wagon, hold him up and probe the soft fat beneath the pinfeathers with their dark, bony fingers and they would kiyi and go at it – a noise that delighted us.

There was a small house on one of the side streets down there. The door was on the street level but the house run down into the lot. Those Chinamen would walk up and just put their hand on the door and it would open. We tried but it was locked. We sat across the street and tried to decipher how those Chinamen got in and finally I figured there was a guy inside watchin' who would open up when the right one come along.

Well, one Sunday the Salvation Army held a street meetin' down in Chinatown. The band was playin' in front of that little house. Different ones would take the tambourine around for donations. They gave it to Jessie. She went through the crowd toward that little house. When the door opened she slipped in. I hear a big commotion goin' on so I busted in. They was shovin' Jessie out the door. Her tambourine was piled with money. When we got home she told us that it was real dark and smelled funny. Said it was just some old men layin' around on cots, smokin'. Some kind of social club, I guess.

The Christmas after Pa died some folks from the Elks came to our house up on Ralston Hill. Of course when Mom opened the door we all pushed around her to see what was goin' on. There were two women standing on our porch. One handed a basket to Mom, the other gave one to me. It was heavy with food and toys wrapped up in fancy Christmas paper, all decorated with tinsel and foil bells hangin' down. I can still remember how it smelled of ham, spicy like cinnamon and cloves. Well, you know kids, oh boy! But before we could touch a thing Mom said in the softest voice, "I'm afraid you've made a mistake. There's a family right up the road in a white house, they could really use these things." And she handed the basket back to the woman. I did the same. They just stood there a moment lookin' at us — Mom and us kids like a wreath around her. That was Christmas enough for me.

Jessie

The doctor told me, I'll only give your mother a couple of years if she has to work this hard, so I quit school. I was just out of junior high. One of the neighbor ladies said, You're crazy, but I didn't think it was any of her business. I got a job runnin' an elevator eight hours a day, six days a week, and I ironed at night. I ironed jillions of shirts. I never learned to dance. I never went with anybody. But I thought, that's all right. Mom was just doin' what she could.

Jessie

Mom always said, In this country you don't need towels. You get out of the tub, maybe shake a little, then by the time you clean up the bathroom you're all dry. You don't need a towel.

Margaret Langston Bariski

*They were wild and woolly and full of fleas
and never been curried below the knees.
The man ain't alive that can get the job done yet.*

In 1926 Mom heard that Neill West, owner of the ⊞
Ranch three miles southeast of Sparks, was hiring wran-
glers. She asked me if I would be interested in inquiring
about the job. I was.

West supplied horses for the divorcée dude ranch trade as
well as for his summer camps at both Lake Tahoe and Lake
Donner. I jumped at a chance to ditch my delivery bike and
go back to work on a ranch with horses. That was where I
met Bud Blundell and Paul Fite. West had just bought sixty
head of good saddle horses to supply his dude business.
Shorty, Shaska West, and Paul were shoeing the cavvy when
I hired on. That first year I worked in the shop or ran
errands, whatever there was to do. I didn't have too much to
do with the horses. I just ran the forge. Shaska and Paul did
all the fittin' of the shoes.

One day old West told me, If you'll stay here and hay for
me this summer, I'll give you a vacation on pay. I didn't care
what I was doin', as long as I had a job, so I told him that
was fine. I drove a team of mules on a rake. Gin and Red,
two sorrel mules. Boy, they was goers, I tell you.

But when I finished the hayin' West sent me up to the girls' camp on the west shore of Lake Tahoe to pick up a horse that had been giving 'em trouble. He was a big bay horse with a white face that run around on his jaws and he was a son-of-a-gun to shy. I guess he'd probably whirled out from under some of the girls so West sent me up there on another horse to trade and I rode the bay horse back. He was a pretty bugger, too, but he'd see something goin' down the road and you'd be headed back the other way pretty darned quick.

They was havin' a rodeo at Lake Tahoe when I come by. A regular rodeo, a big one. West furnished all the horses, so of course Bud and Paul were there. That Paul was a ripper. He'd ride broncos and look back over his shoulder at the crowd, all around over the fence, smilin', never look at his horse at all, and ride that bugger to a frazzle.

Bud had his little gray horse, Danny, entered in the stake race. There was probably eight horses in that race. Quite a bunch of 'em lined up, I know. I think every horse in the race could have outrun Danny, but boy! when he got to that stake, why, he'd just drag Bud's leg on the stake gettin' around it. He was about halfway back before the others got stopped. Won it both days plumb easy.

Anyway, after the rodeo was over Bud and I had to take

the horses down the road a mile or so and put 'em in a pasture. Paul grabbed an old pinto horse out of the bunch, jumped on him bareback, and rode along with us, no bridle or nothin'. When we got out to the highway most of the horses had started down the road and we was comin' along behind. This big limousine, as long as a barn, comes up the highway and stops to let the horses go by. There was four ladies in the thing. Had the top folded back, class outfit. That darned Paul seen 'em and just made a beeline for that big car. He run that pinto horse right into the side of the car and when the horse slid to a stop Paul flew right over his head and right into the ladies' laps. The horse trotted along with the bunch and Paul stayed right there in the car. A'course, he was a good-lookin' guy and had a good line, too. I guess those ladies got quite a kick out of him.

Wild West Show Is Big Arena Feature

Reno Gazette Journal, August 15, 1927

Bronzed men and women from the ranges and plains of Nevada and other Western states are vieing with one another in giving visitors to Nevada's Transcontinental Highways Exposition real thrills in the Wild West performances in the main arena every afternoon and evening.

This feature of the exposition, which furnishes a real touch of the old West, is being put on under the direction of Neill West, native of Nevada, who for two months before the exposition opened, scoured the country for the best riders and bunch of bucking horses that he could gather.

Among the riders are Paul Fite, noted bull dogger and all round rider, formerly of New Mexico, now on the T. H. ranch at Pyramid lake. Bud Blundell of Rodeo Creek, near Wadsworth, is a Nevadan. Silvan Morrow of Calgary, Canada, who has shown at numerous rodeos and won his spurs in many a contest, gives an exhibition of bulldogging and sticks some of the worst buckers.

Young Barnsby, a Sacramento boy, has shown class in sticking on wild mules, cows, steers and horses while George Morgan, a Pyramid lake Indian, gave the crowd a thrill after thrill last night when he stayed to the limit on a mule that changed ends, sun-fished and tried every known trick to unseat its rider. Several times it looked as though the mule would win but finally it gave up and loped off and Morgan jumped off amid the plaudits of the crowd. "Slim" Langston of Duke

Lake and Tommy Harris of Honey Lake, both all-round riders and bull doggers are other stars to be seen beneath the big top.

One of the real events of the Wild West show is the stage hold-up. The old stage coach used in this scene is the one driven by Hank Monk from Carson to Lake Tahoe during the early days of the West. Driven by a pioneer, the stage coach is stopped by a band of war decorated Indians and just as the passengers are lined-up by the red men, whoops and pistol shots are heard and a bunch of cow boys dash down the arena putting the Indians to route.

From the time first buckers are turned from the corral until the program ends there is not a draggy moment and with the performance put on to music by the exposition band, zest is added to the riders, the horses and the crowd.

Three professionals participate in the show. They win plaudits of the crowd at every appearance. They are Bonny Gray, who jumps her horse over an automobile filled with people and does trick and fancy riding. Sam Garrett, world champion roper, who makes his lariat seem like a living thing. Ed Wright, the cowboy clown, and his trained mule, are a real feature of the show.

Brin

The brindle cow wandered at will feeding on her choice of the season. Her domain was a meadow beyond the rock barn, the horse pasture, it was called. One wrangle horse and a favored mare and foal were her companions, along with the buggy horses in case the boss wanted to hook them to his light oak cart, which he bought from the Pacheco Wagon Works five hundred miles away, at the base of Mount Diablo. Every spring he tied the black mare to the back of the cart and went off to the best Standardbred stallion in the country. She never missed a year breeding up. Her foals of other years were his fine cart horses and broke out like silk. Disposition, he believed, rested with the dam.

When snow layered on ice the brindle cow ate summer hay forked from a stack in the center of the pasture. She took her leisure on a high bank above the creek and drank water running where the men chopped ice, or she pulled to a dry corner out of the wind. In spring the foal of the favored mare found her in the shade of the black willow where a red-tailed hawk nested, where a small pale barn owl spent afternoons, dropping dark, furry plugs of field mice and voles among the roots lifted twisting, rubbed doorknob smooth by Brin's long neck. The foal came close to smell at her while she loafed, chewing her cud, walked around her haunch to horn, trembling nostrils blowing small puffs of breath against the cow's neck, ear, temple, eye.

Twice a day, early chores and late, the woman came from the

house with her shining pail. By now the many cups of the separator were scalded and set in their proper sequence to catch each heavy drop of cream. Her milk appeared in every variety of batter, gravy, pudding, and sauce, but the cream was, well, the cream of the boss's meal, welling ladle turning strong coffee tan. Thick gold cream – for butter and whipped cream to be spooned over oatmeal or cobbler – would not spill from an inverted jar.

The brindle cow, jersey, mostly, with the deep dark eyes of the breed, was the same age of her eldest son and calved from her third year on, often with the woman, their gestations being equal. The only time she showed temper was on her cycle. The woman recognized tension in her own hands and talked while she set a pan of oats down on the meadow and, making herself a three-legged stool – two legs of her own and the single spiked leg of the milking stool – balanced beside the heavy udder.

It was an easing time for the woman. No other women for miles, for months. It wasn't just their conversation she missed – most women could talk ranching right along with the men. A woman's voice was more like music how it moved from word to word, folding, you might say, around each word, sliding easy, the nature of water taking her along in the steady glide. One spoke of how her toddler napped in a box with the kittens, or how clouds frothed pink above the snowy mountains, or the yardage of tartan plaid found in the bottom of the sewing trunk she'd intended for a waistcoat, smocked into dresses for the girls. And there were silences, head down, shoulders, back, sturdy arms kneading dough, or peeling the blush off Bellflower apples, or grating cabbage into a bowl just across the room, normally empty of all but her and the stove waiting wood, and the family wanting supper. She cherished gatherings at the old fort on Summit Lake, carts and horses tied on the parade grounds, men fishing the lake for cutthroat trout to cook on green willow sticks before an evening fire, or in one's winter kitchen, or on a Sunday picnic and horseshoe pitching on Aspen Creek. And she longed for the comfort of laughter rising – bread resting by the stove pushing the dish towel smooth – her belly as her child grew.

The brindle cow's flank, the smell of her changed with where she laid, sage and rabbit brush beyond the creek, or willow, clover, manure, all of it on top of the smell of her being cow and her dark hide, a mottled blur of tan and gold – the taffeta gown she wore when she met her man. In the hide there were pictures: a bird's head, a family crest, a backward stare of eyes, a nose hooked into an old man's cane, a musical staff and spots – notes she made into a song. At the warmth of this flank she took some time to wander free and no one would break in or come near. The men were glad she took the chore. When she was ill with the seventh child, her eldest son took her outside work: the hens, rabbits she raised for pelts and meat, the calf pen, chopping wood. And the old cow would not stand for him. He hit her with the stool and slapped her and cussed her good but finally threw the stool and pail down and made a hobbles out of rope to stop her mincing steps. She fought the hobbles. When the woman was well enough – before she was well enough – she felt her anger's flood at the deep burns inside the bend of hock. It took bacon grease and turpentine and most of spring to heal them.

Mainly she saw things from the old cow's flank she had no other time to see: sagging fences that needed tending, pruning in the orchard she must take time to do, shadows on the far hills, storms that hit up high and smelled of snow, desert bluebirds that flashed a wing the color of her baby's eyes.

When the cow lay dead – curled, her head back along her side – she knew it was coming. She watched her eldest boy working with the men and couldn't tell him back-to. Watery milk dwindled with just a skim of cream. One of her heifer calves had been saved back from sale and bred to freshen before the rhubarb came. He dearly loved cream on rhubarb pie.

She knew the men would take her hide. It was perfect for braiding, no break of color to weaken strings. They had been eyeing her as her hip bones peaked like tent poles, she became more skeleton than cow, and they took to calling her Old Rawhide. The young one, Slim, could braid a riata in short a week, standing, bundles – he called them tamales – thick as fists dangling, pulling each strand straight, even as the last, backing up with the length growing through his gloved hands.

They dragged the carcass off to the dead pile out in the greasewoods, not so far away the woman couldn't see ravens and magpies dive into the brush, coyotes slip out of the deep draw at dusk. But before Slim took the hide down and laid his bone-handled knife to the grain she went out to the barn. Big as a blanket, it pulled tear-shaped holes against the heads of nails. She ran her hand over a cat's arched back, dull flare of sunrise, the man's hooked cane, and hummed the notes that made Brin's song.

Shadows on the far hills

Trailing to Piedmont, California

West kept me busy shuffling horses between the headquarters and the lakes, and packing boys into the mountains from the camp near Glenbrook on Lake Tahoe, and then, a different kind of job came my way.

The second year I worked for West, a millionaire named Phair bought two horses from him. Bayou was a big buckskin horse and the other was a bay-and-white pinto horse called Dan. Phair was gonna have 'em shipped on the train down to Piedmont, California, but for some reason decided to have 'em rode down instead. 'Course I didn't know anything about the deal. West had promised me a vacation on pay, but when this came up, why, he volunteered me to go. He said, Just take your time. Don't hurry. Thirty miles a day is plenty.

This Mr. Phair bought a brand-new outfit, saddle, bridle, everything new. He got a pack saddle to put on the pinto. I rode the buckskin most of the time. And he bought blankets to put on the horses at night. Old cow horses! They never had a blanket on in their lives, so I never used 'em at all. Didn't figure I needed 'em, but they were along anyway.

I started out from Lake Tahoe, at the girls' camp, and I crossed the mountain to a place called Rubicon Springs. The country was full of big rocks, big boogers that shined when the sun was on them. I don't know what kind of rock, but pretty and just everywhere. I camped there that night. The next day I hit the main road and followed it. I think I made it to Folsom and I camped there. The next day it was eighteen miles to Sacramento. On the outskirts of town I run into a place where they had a big camp set to get horses ready for the state fair. There was circus or carnival outfit set up there, too. I hunted around and found the boss and he said I was welcome to stay there with 'em that night, so I did. Real nice folks.

From there I went through Sacramento toward Vallejo. I had to cross the Sacramento River on a ferry. I was lucky and got there just as the ferry pulled out with a load of automobiles. That was what they was mainly ferryin', I guess. When the old guy that was runnin' the show got ready to load the ferry, he put me and the horses up front so I could get off first and I wouldn't have to eat the smoke from all the automobiles puttin' off. I guess the horses was nervous from the motion of the boat. They would grab each other, and their teeth just snapped! I finally had to get between 'em to keep 'em apart. My gosh, they'd bite hard!

I was supposed to phone him when I got to Berkeley and

he would come and lead me into his place. Well, I knew how to use a telephone but I musta done somethin' wrong 'cause I never could get anybody to answer. So I thought, Heck with this, I'll go on. I can find that place. And there was no mistaking it when I got there. They had a great big thing across the street that said Piedmont. It was a special section of the city, I guess. I went to a service station to find out the direction of Mr. Phair's house and I rode in just about dusk.

Phair was there and he took me out to his private stable. He had two horses stabled there and one empty stall for Bayou. He had a stableman hired and all he did was take care of those horses. He led 'em out to show 'em to me. One was a dark bay, and man, you could see yourself in his hide! Geez, that booger did shine! The other one was a real light bay, almost a buckskin. We took old Dan to a big stable right down the road. They had over a hundred head of private saddle horses in that stable. Why, it was like walkin' in a hotel! Door and rooms, heck, you didn't see a horse in that place. We walked down through there and he got 'em to lead out one or two to show me, these fancy five- or seven-gaited ones. Fancy! We left old Dan there. I would've liked to have seen him in a month. Probably wouldn't recognize him.

There was no train back to Reno until the next night. The next day Mr. Phair took me over to San Francisco on the ferry. While he went to his office I took one of those sight-seeing buses and spent the day on one of those tours. The driver was pointin' things out as we went along and in one part of town the wash was hangin' across the street on clotheslines and he said, "Look, the flags of every nation." That's the one special thing I remember about that day.

It took me eight days goin' down. When I left Mr. Phair gave me fifty dollars for expense money. When I got down there I had five dollars left. He let me keep it and gave me an extra forty-five. He put me on the train home and I was back in Reno the next morning.

Hardscrabble. That's what they called the place.

Love Wears a Blind Bridle

Lige tipped his hat to me the first time we met. I knew by John's manner when he introduced us that the tall man was someone special. After that, if I chanced on him at the post office or on the sidewalk, his head would come down, his right hand up to his hat, the soft felt creased by this habit of respect. All his warm greetings in later years were anchored in that first gesture.

It wasn't that easy with everyone. Until 1970 I thought I was invisible. My life had been spent in the country but on the cut fringe of the East Bay, neighborhoods, freeways, miles of shopping centers, developments popping up like radishes in a garden row, and everyone living their own style in anonymity. When I announced my plans to move to Surprise Valley my father advised me to keep my nose clean. I would have been better served had he said, Take your heart but leave your miniskirt in San Francisco.

I missed the *Chronicle*. The *Modoc Record* is a weekly. I missed KSFO's morning D.J., Donny Babe. Modoc's local radio station airs "The School Lunch Menu" and "The Funeral Report." I missed that unconditional acceptance of family and friends, not having to prove anything, going my way supported but unnoticed. When you're an outsider in Modoc it's as obvious as your brand on someone else's calf.

John teased that when he married me he was bringing new blood into the valley the way all ranchers introduce genetic diversity into their herds. I was secretly convinced that on a given day in the near future a wedding would take place and every house the length of the valley would shudder in an explosive chain reaction locking together like Legos, everyone finally related, once and for all.

Surprise Valley is isolated, but I was isolated in a larger sense from the women. Most of them, like Kay, worked endlessly keeping the house and garden and the family functioning in good order and left the ranch work to the men and kids. The ones who worked outside doing ranch work had no time to hold my hand. I had been riding all my life and I wanted nothing more than to ride alongside John every day. Sitting before the mangle ironing sheets and fingertip towels, finding yet another way to unmold Jell-O salad, eradicating buttonweed from the face of the earth were not the things of myth. Riding under a grand open sky behind cows spilling off a sidehill like springwater was. I made no effort to involve myself in women's social functions. Kay could see I was tracking up the smooth face of convention. When my birthday rolled around she asked me out to lunch. Lunch just happened to be the fall meeting of the Cowbelles, the women's auxiliary of the Modoc County Cattlemen's Association. She handed me a receipt at the door – my dues paid up for a year. Right off I had a problem with the name, Cowbelles. I thought they were kidding. Horsewomen would never allow themselves to be tagged the Mare Band. Kay assured me it was better than being called a BoPeep or a Porkette.

I attended meetings regularly until plans for the Cattleman of the Year banquet were being discussed. Even as a newcomer I knew of several women who managed their own operations and deserved the honor so I suggested we nominate a woman rancher for the award. The gasp nearly sucked the glass out of the windows. Clearly the ERA movement could not look to the Cowbelles for support. I can't remember if they blackballed me but I never went to another meeting. I had no one to blame but myself. (Actually, twenty years later the Modoc County Cattlemen's Association bestowed their highest award on Juanita Gardner, and the Cowbelles changed their name to Cattlewomen. There's a price to pay, being a visionary.)

I eventually learned that the witty quips and insider gossip of Herb Caen and Donny Babe had no relevance to Surprise Valley. I had to get on or get off of the horse. I couldn't get anything done dragging around with one foot in the stirrup. It took a lot of faith in John to let go but I began to understand the character of my new home. If I figure the county population the way ranchers do carrying capacity of livestock, we are .42 people to the square mile. I admit that calculation includes a lot of public land, but still . . . When you're that scattered and the newspaper comes only once a week, it's important to have the livestock market report, community news and calendar of events, yard sales, feedstore specials, school field trips, and ball scores, as well as funeral announcements, on the radio. Modoc is a large county with a small population and we live with the paradox of the sideview mirror – being further away yet nearer. That being so, the responsibility for community welfare rests equally on us and we have learned to employ the first rule of housekeeping. If I don't pick it up, who will? There's no faceless government in control. We forced the California Department of Water Resources to support us in a ten-year-long battle to stop Reno's water grab scheme along our county/state border and on our permitted grazing land in Nevada. We wrote a grant to bring

PBS television into an unserved rural area. We marched on the county courthouse when the California Department of Corrections announced the release of a serial rapist to Modoc and our governor explained to the press, "Well, no one lives up there." We forced the county supervisors to put a proposed prison on the ballot, defeated the measure, and now live with the hard feelings between those who saw the prison as a boost to the economy and those who compared it to living alongside a nuclear dump site. We know the phone numbers of our legislative aides and they know ours. When something needs tending, from sweeping up the streets before the fair and burning vacant lots before fire season to grassroots activism, people band together across the boundaries of political and cultural platforms. That's how I found the women I needed. They were there all the time, doing their own work but coming together to protect the whole. Their welcome was as deep and genuine as Lige tipping his hat.

Winter is when we find time for each other, not regularly, but the telephone rings and cars pull up here, at Bettie's, Sophie's, Lynette's, Kathy's. Women carrying spinning wheels and baskets of clean wool gather around and spin out yarns fine and strong as friendship. The swish of the wheels soothes us. Great raging conversations stir us. I suspect some don't even care about the wool but love the idea that one fleece keeps many warm. People who don't understand what's happening would like to pigeonhole us: ranch women, old hippies, newcomers, flatlanders, government lice, tree huggers, but we won't go for it. We're just women who love this valley in all its diversity.

The night of January 1, 1997, a debris flow swept down out of Powley Canyon and covered all of Bettie and Joe Parman's ranch except for about forty-five acres. Barns, shop, some of their cattle, trucks, stock trailers, haying equipment, Bettie's green houses, their home, their daughter's and son-in-law's home, in short all they had built in their fifty years of marriage was under an estimated four million tons of mountainside. Old growth timber with roots twisted like Q-tips and rocks as big as travel trailers dwarfed what was left of Bettie's house. Two trees eighteen inches in diameter speared it like a shish kebob. The kitchen sink was found a half mile from the house. A tree lay across the hole in the counter where it had been. Geologists expert in land movement call it a classic debris flow. The warm storm that liquefied the snow pack caused damage the length of the valley but none to the extent of the Parmans'.

People gathered at the Lake City Fire Hall to see how we could help. We knew they were lucky to get out with their lives, but standing at the edge of the rubble, seeing the destruction, the house blown open by the power of the nature, and our dear friend Bettie leading the expedition to get out the "most important things," we all got a lesson in strength. About a hundred yards from the house were her three freezers. I guess you have to understand Bettie. She always worries about people being hungry or in need, and she has a passion to create, anything, everything: sew, build, pot, plant, spin, knit, weave, paint, cook. If it can go in a jar, she will by God put it there, or dry it or pickle it or freeze it. When they tipped the first freezer upright and opened the lid there were stacks of Bettie's pies, pretty as the day they were made. Her Lake City Garden was a rock garden now, but the fruit she produced last year was in those pie pans. "I guess I'll have to sell those pies to make some money. The insurance sure as hell ain't gonna give us anything," she said. Her spinning pals she had named the Surprise Valley Garden Club and Vigilante Corps took her at her word. We offered her pies at a minimum price of one hundred dollars and raised over twenty thousand dollars. The money came from everywhere but the bulk of it came from right close to home, from other folks who don't have extra but were willing to share what they could with their friends.

But money wasn't the only gift. There were gifts of food and time. Through January, February, March stray cars were parked at the Parmans' fenceline and bits of their possessions were dug out of the frozen mud. They found Bettie's silver bridle, but not Joe's. Lynn took Bettie's computer and copy machine to his shop and painstakingly cleaned and repaired them. That sort of thing. In April they bought a house in Lake City and people came to help paint and get them moved in. On Valentine's Day we held a pie social at the Community Church and invited everyone to come by for pie and coffee so Bettie could thank them formally. She wept without shame. "I didn't know so many people loved us."

I can't think of Bettie without remembering an afternoon in her old house. She toured me through her ceramics classroom upstairs where kids and grownups come to pour, fire, glaze, and paint greenware under her direction. "Come here, Lindy, I want to show you something," she said and pulled a box out with eight hand-painted tiles – roses, half-opened daisies, trailing wisteria, and her name. She laid them out on the table. They joined in a spring garden scene – her burial headstone. "You can see there's no date on it yet," she laughed. "I'm thinking about framing it and hanging it on the wall so I can enjoy it now."

One side of Surprise Valley is mountains, forest, and fertile meadows that feed the animals that feed us. The other side is in the rain shadow – high desert, spacious, silent, nourishing in another way. Between them is the lake. Many think the alkaline water spoiled, wasted, but if you go out on the causeway there is a different view. Avocets, willets, teal fly up from the lake that separates the two mountain ranges and binds them in a reflection with the sky.

Modoc County, named the bellwether county of the state, has a rich history within easy reach. In 1849 an estimated twenty thousand people crossed through what was later quartered off as Modoc County, lured to the promised riches of fertile Oregon valleys or California's gold fields. The trail forked on the west side of the Warners and so did the stories. In 1852 there was an Indian massacre of sixty-four pioneers at Bloody Point. Twenty years later the only major Indian war fought in California, the Modoc War, broke out. The battle took place at Captain Jack's Stronghold, a maze of lava tubes and caves in the Lava Beds National Monument. Fifty Modoc warriors held off nearly one thousand soldiers at a cost to the U.S. government in excess of one million dollars and the lives of several hundred civilians and soldiers. In 1905 the *San Francisco Chronicle* reported on the hideous hanging of four men and a boy from the Lookout bridge with the banner "Modoc's Done It Again." They were called an outlaw band, accused of petty theft and malicious mischief. Evidence implicated a vigilante group, some members were tried, but no real convictions were handed down. And in 1911 Modoc County made national headlines when the brutal murder of four Surprise Valley stockmen was discovered in Nevada's Little High Rock Canyon. There was a long history attached to the High Grade gold mines on Bidwell Mountain, of holdups, a woman freighter by the name Buckskin Annie, boosterism, and the investor W. P. Wrigley, the chewing gum king.

But my interest was not in the sensational stories. It was, and is, in the smaller, personal, human stories; why others chose, as I recently had, to live in this ranching community isolated in the corner of the state. I discovered a way to learn about the families and the traditions of the county at the first meeting of the Modoc County Historical Society. A speaker read a list of Modocers who had died the previous year. People in the audience offered what they knew of the lost history buried with them. We needed the information firsthand and it was urgent we begin gathering the oral histories of our elders. I signed out a tape recorder and a stack of tapes.

I thought it best to practice on someone I knew, someone who shared common interests, someone easy to talk to. I telephoned Lige. Etta answered the phone. I cuddled her along thinking it would make her at ease with what I intended proposing to her husband. After a while I asked to speak to Lige. She held the phone out and yelled, "Lige! Telephone! It's that Linda Hussa. If she wants you to go some place, don't you go!" Pretty soon Lige picked up the phone. His voice came warm and strong. I asked how he was. "Oh, just percolatin' along." I asked if I could interview him about braiding rawhide. He said, "Well, I don't know what I can tell you, but I guess so." I said if we could do it at our house, I'd pick him up in a few minutes. "I'll be ready," he sang out. And he was.

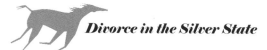

Divorce in the Silver State

I work on a dude ranch near Reno,
　Givin' thrills to these divorce-seeking dames,
Every morning it's a splittin' headache,
　Every night it's one or more flames.

One was a lady from Frisco,
　One was a gal from Spo-kain,
One was the wife of a guy servin' life,
　Another was a gay one from Maine.

A gay young divorcée, she won me,
　Seekin' love in the West for a change,
Now I'm a gigolo in spurs, and the fault is all hers;
　Gosh, I wish I was back on the range!

Anon.

Nevada is the Separation State: the Great Basin separates the Sierra Nevada Mountains from the Wasatch, the miners began separating Nevada's mineral wealth from her rocky soil in the mid-1800s, gamblers and joy houses separated the miner from his poke, and at the turn of the century, the law separated better from worse.

The United States took a hard stand on marriage, probably firmer than on any other contract binding human intent. The eternity of marriage was supported by church, state, and society, and its failure was discouraged. But fail it did, and when it did, divorce was administered by each state's cumbersome legal process.

The Silver State presented a solution to dissolution without knowing it, and the dust has not yet settled. Nevada's mining gypsies rolled like quicksilver on plate glass, following rumors of rich strikes from one claim to another. When statehood was given to the territory in 1864 the residency requirement was set at six months to advantage the miner in the right to vote. Residency of more than six months would have left the question of politics to a very few eligible voters in a wandering population.

It was through this residency loophole that a New York attorney slipped his client at the turn of the century. The Nevada opportunity made national headlines in 1905 when Laura Corey, the wife of William Corey, president of United States Steel, moved to Reno and supplied the newspapers with the details of her husband's philandering while she waited out the six month period. In Mrs. Corey's home state, divorce was granted only on proof of adultery. Nevada developed a more reasonable attitude in regard to dissolving marriage vows, once the benefits became evident, and validated multiple-choice complaints: adultery, cruelty, desertion, nonsupport, alcoholism, felony, impotency, five years' separation without cohabitation, or five years of insanity. The Silver State loosened the corset strings of society's Victorian rules and opened its door to the painless divorce.

The word was out. Ads for Nevada's easy divorce appeared in New York newspapers and theater programs with offers for pamphlets "free on request." For the next decade Reno was the desert oasis where the unresolvable problems of marriage could be set right. The men stayed home and tended to business while the women brought the money and came west.

Women of position and wealth were not satisfied with the working-class shopping the sagebrush city had to offer. If they were forced to cool their heels in the sticks for six long months they wanted to enjoy the stay. Reno responded with finery never seen before in the Truckee Meadows. Fashionable shops opened in town showing jewelry, gowns, and expensive furs in their storefront windows. Restaurants, night spots, salons, and car dealerships followed the hot strike. Nevada gave birth to miners of a new breed. It was not the intention of Nevada's founding fathers to turn their state into the divorce mecca of the nation, but the law accommodated the need and it became clear that "there was gold in them thar frills."

This aspect of economics was celebrated until the moral crusade consolidated their demands on the state legislature in 1913.

During an impetuous attack of conscience lawmakers were goaded into extending the residency requirement to one year. A year was too long for eastern society's grand dames to be stuck in a dusty western cowtown even to rid themselves of a marital pain. Other states had amended their laws to compete with Nevada's divorce market, and like the mining camps that crumbled back into the desert, Reno became a ghost town. Tumbleweeds blew down the streets. Elegant shops closed. Voters lost their jobs. Unhappy constituents stormed the capitol, but nothing could be done for two years when the legislature took up again. It didn't take two years for Nevada's population to place the blame. Not one legislator who voted for the twelve-month residency extension in 1913 was reelected to office.

The opportunity made available by Nevada's original residency requirement altered society's attitude toward marriage and divorce. Nevada politicians obliged the philosophy with tolerance and its courts heard uncontested cases with a casual attitude. Other states responded. In 1931 Idaho and Arkansas reduced their residency requirement to three months. The Nevada legislature called their bet by chopping the requirement to six weeks and specifying that divorce cases be tried behind closed doors. Then they upped the ante by sanctioning wide-open gambling. Nevada rode the dark horse of prosperity into the future, and the debt was due to the itinerant miner.

Lawyers met the trains called the "Divorcée Special." Some women preferred the elegance of hotels but others were attracted to the western glamour of dude ranches. Handsome young men in cowboy duds swept up to the depot in the ranch station wagon and while they tied the luggage on drawled promises meant to brighten the desert nights. One bunch of cowboy bell-

hops wore sweaters designed for the Lazy Me Ranch, nick-
named by the local press as the Lay Me Easy Ranch.

Real ranches took in a few guests on the side to help pay the
bills, and the experience did provide an honest look at ranching
for women who didn't require pampering. Neill West and his
wife expanded the Ⴀ Dude Ranch to include a place about thirty miles from Reno on the northwest shore of Pyramid Lake,
where they accommodated a limited number of women and
kept a few young buckaroos around to accompany the guests
on the trail. West moved Bud and Lige out to the Ⴀ and gave
them a string of horses to gentle and ladies to herd.

Lazy Me Ranch

The Ⱶ

After you got to Sutcliff you went north around Pyramid Lake and up the canyon about three miles to the Hardscrabble. That's what they called the place. It had belonged to Flannigan and Dunn sometime or other. Mom had worked for Dunn on the Smoke Creek Desert when she first came to the country. It wasn't much of a ranch but Ⱶ was the brand he put on the horses.

Pert near all the boarders they took in were women who had come to Nevada for a divorce. They'd have a regular cabin and a saddle horse furnished by the ranch. They could ride or whatever they wanted to do.

The first two came out together from New York State, I think. Jo Washington and Bessie. Jo was a good-lookin' gal and a nice gal but she could drink more whiskey than a mule could pack. You couldn't tell it either. She was always dressed western style. She wore a pair of chaps and a neckerchief around her neck. Bessie dressed in the eastern style, chokebore britches and leggin's.

There were three cabins in a group with a porch that joined them all. They had an old carpenter out there named Charlie Addis that could saw out a cabin in the morning, all the boards, then put it together in the afternoon. He worked alone. Quite a carpenter.

Bud and his brother, Ira, decided to start their own dude ranch. Their place was about twenty miles from the ⊦. They started from scratch over there, too. All they had was a two-room cabin, corrals, barn, and a cellar. There wasn't any other buildings. They called it the Monte Cristo.

I was still workin' for the ⊦ when two gals came out from New York to the ranch. We called one of 'em Jerkwater Jones. I don't even remember her real name. The other was Phyllis Felt. After they'd been there awhile they caught Mrs. West goin' through their mail and they moved back into Reno. About the same time Bud asked me if I'd go to work for him and take care of his cattle, so I quit West and moved to the Monte Cristo. That's where I met up with Dad Hicks. It was just him and me feedin' cows that winter, just the two of us, together.

Bud had met Phyllis at a dance at Flanigan and was kind of sweet on her, so she and Jerkwater Jones started coming out to the Monte Cristo. I don't remember how they got word to me but I had to meet 'em down below the ranch three or four miles with a buckboard and team. You couldn't get in there with a car. They'd stay a week or so at a time. Bud wasn't even there then. He was out north of Lovelock runnin' the horses he fell heir to after his mother died, but he did come in and stayed the winter. By then, Phyllis and Jerk-water Jones were livin' at the Monte Cristo full-time.

They didn't have electricity or running water at the Monte Cristo. They had one kitchen for everybody in the main house. At first they wanted everybody up for breakfast but they found out pretty fast that that wouldn't work. Those ladies weren't used to gettin' up early so they worked it into kind of a short-order kitchen. They had a fella there that was a good cook. He could make the best hotcakes I ever tasted. I wanted to watch how he made those hotcakes and I got up way early one morning, but he had them all mixed and was just beatin' the heck out of 'em. I even asked him for the recipe and he just laughed. Wouldn't give it to me. One of the ladies asked for it and he gave it to her but I think she had to give him twenty dollars for it.

Bud and Ira ran around four or five hundred head of cattle out on the range year-round. My job was to take care of them. I did quite a lot of buckarooin', 'cause the cattle would work down onto the Indian reservation and I was suppose to keep 'em off. There was one bunch in particular that I had to move pretty regular and shove 'em back up above the headquarters of the Monte Cristo. When I got back up to the house that day Phyllis asked me how I got down that hill. Did you go down there ahorseback? she asked. I told her, Yes, I had to get down off there. She said, I wouldn't think about ridin' downhill. And I said, Aw, you buckaroo with me a month, you'll go anyplace. So she started ridin' with me and she got to be pretty good help. It wasn't long after that she was helpin' me take a bunch up the road and one old unruly cow in the bunch bailed off into this little draw. It was pretty darned steep but Phyllis bailed off after her. Heck! I had to laugh. I told her, "You're doin' pretty good for somebody who wouldn't ride downhill." We gave her a little red bay horse they called Firefly. That was her horse.

Blundell's got two other gals to stay right off that first winter. Mary Shippen and a gal named Cumberland. I run around with the Cumberland gal. She was a big tall gal, single and up towards thirty. She came to kinda chaperone this Mary, 'cause Mary was only about nineteen and gettin' a divorce.

Mary knew horses, trained race horses and jumpin' horses. If there was a blemish on a horse, by golly, she'd find it, now. She bought a mare from Bud. A tall, slim gray mare, a range-raised five-year-old. She said this buckin' business was a lot of baloney. Should be against the rules. So she was gonna show all of us. There was a guy livin' at the Monte Cristo, old Lee Rivers. He'd been gassed in the war and he couldn't stand to be inside. He had to be out in the open with the fresh air all the time. He was just an old cowboy, was all he was. He took up with these dudes, and after Mary bought this mare, Lee was helpin' break her to ride. They had to start in right from scratch 'cause she'd never been handled.

Well, they fooled around there for two or three weeks, or a month maybe, got her halter broke, and saddled her up. Mary would get on and Lee would lead her ahorseback. He had some gentle horses of this own. They did that for quite a while, but the first day they turned her loose, she bucked Mary off.

Mary wore corduroy britches and the mare stepped on her leg and tore about an eight-inch slit in her pants. Well, that was the first thing I noticed when I came in that day, was this rip in Mary's pants. She told us she got bucked off. She had been givin' us quite a time about these horses buckin' so we took right after her then. That was the last time she rode the mare. She just give it up. She found out that that buckin' wasn't against the rules.

Monte Cristo Ranch

Thirty-five miles from Reno, in Washoe County . . . overlooking beautiful Pyramid Lake . . . unsurpassed scenery.

Come and Rough-it Comfortably at A Real Western Cow Ranch

Rates $7.00 a Day or $165 a Month. Reductions for two or more in one cabin. Rates include private cabin, board, and personal saddle horse.

Pack Trips with Cowboy Guides, Mountain Hiking, Picnics, Rodeos, Riding, Swimming, Fishing, Croquet, Archery. Instruction in Riding if necessary.

Monte Cristo Ranch

Address
BLUNDELL BROS.
P. O. Box 380 - Sparks, Nevada
or
P. O. Box 999 - Reno, Nevada

New York City about 3,000 miles ⟶

They built a big dance hall up at the Monte Cristo. It had a pretty good floor in it, I guess, 'cause when you'd come in the door Bud'd be waitin' with a hammer right there to drive all the tacks up in your boots so you wouldn't scratch his floor too bad. One night this one gal named Murphy was standin' over by the phonograph and I don't know what she did but she slipped and fell down. She lit just sittin'! It shook the building! I didn't see it but I heard it, all right. She got up and said, I'll never be the same after that!

She could drink more whiskey than a mule could pack.

Paul Fite

I was goin' from Mom's back out to the Monte Cristo right by Paul's place, so I rode over to pay him a visit. Paul had a little cabin off the main road to Pyramid Lake about a quarter of a mile. I monkeyed around in the yard waterin' my horse at the tank, even hollered, but nobody showed up. I had the feeling he was in the house. Something made me think that. But he wouldn't come out.

He had got in pretty deep with Mrs. Neill West. I guess he was kinda monkeyin' around with her and she developed an awful crush on him. A couple of weeks before at a doin's out at Flannigan she asked him to dance. She followed him around all night. Paul tried to ditch her but she wouldn't back off so he went into the men's room and crawled out the window.

I heard he sold all his cattle and left the country. I never saw him after that. He just kinda disappeared.

The Tree on Bitner Rim

It is said, "Plant a juniper by your door.
Before a witch can enter every leaf must
be correctly counted."

Juniper trees, lowly cousin to the lofty cedar, are not among my favorites. They have no grace at all, no sweep of the fernlike pine, no willowing branches, no whisper, no music as they follow the wind. The juniper is a tree for pioneers. Tough limbs cored with twisted steel cable will spring back a welting slap, roguish twigs will catch and cut, and you will wear its pitch until you're old and gray. They grow anywhere, any way, on rocks or crags, with water or not. If the seed in the frosty blue berry touches down on dirt, a prickly stem will grow and cling despite the odds. Wild fires kept them trimmed and high up in the early days – so it says in photographs – and pioneers had to work for firewood and posts. They hacked out roads in canyons and set up wood camps to labor out loads of heavy green juniper to fuel their winter keep. Teetering wagon roads run out rocky slopes above the valley to ashy stumps of grand old junipers fallen with a cross-cut saw. Modern forest management has fostered an age of pyro-paranoia and the juniper took the "no fire" stance as a blessing. Now the foothills are grizzled with them.

The Paiute have a story about juniper trees, and of course, Coyote plays a part.

At the beginning First People prepared to plant the earth with trees. The tedious work of sorting the seeds was nearly finished when Coyote came trotting up. He wanted to help but they hesitated, knowing he was careless and lazy. They ignored him but he pestered them until they gave in. They handed him a pouch of juniper berries and gave him careful instructions. They told him to dig a hole for each seed and cover them well. They told him to plant the seeds away from other trees as they were greedy and would suck up all the water, growing fat while the pine, the aspen and the willow would shrivel and die. Yes yes, he called over his shoulder. But he wasn't even out of their sight when he gave a laugh, threw a handful of berries into his mouth and spit them out in a garrulous spray. Where the seeds landed a stem sprouted. Coyote went on spitting seeds here and there as he trotted along until the bag was empty and young juniper trees were scattered over the hills of the valley.

I can tolerate junipers in the forest because they do not dominate the desert with their clutter. Mahogany, aspen, cottonwood courteously grow in tidy groups and don't freckle the desert's skin. For now, the open land is still open.

Isn't life hard enough without being so certain? the kindly desert mused, then took my hand and led me to a juniper east of where they're likely found, in the wide and bending basin north of Badger Mountain, where ridges run long and with the compass, north and south. On the morning side of one lava flow a magpie, raven, or crow flew with the bruised blue berry in its gut and dropped it there. At that spot the seed grew weedy. Prickly first growth and pitchy smell did not tempt cow or horse or antelope, any browser or grazer that roams the land. Years gave it into a tree.

On a fall ride I hit the outside swing to push cattle to the Flat, where the herd was building by the mile. I rode every swale and pocket, where water raised or held. My horse pecked along a trail worn on rocks, little more than kinder plates of lava and velvet dirt between. Low brush shuffled around plates shading asters. Grasshoppers spun ahead to clear the way. A quick movement – within shade hanging under the single tree – stopped me. A spreading set of antlers turned slightly, side to side, ears twitched flies away, and a buck drowsed in the warm afternoon. Luck was with me, sound and smell.

I was sure he would explode once he sensed me there but in answer to my hello his head turned, dark eyes drew me in. He rose, arched his back to stretch, to let the tension work his muscles smooth, and sauntered half a circle thirty yards away.

> *Then we talked.*
> *I said, beauty.*
> *He agreed. I said,*
> *I loved his quiet place.*
> *He said, thank you.*
> *There was a pause.*
> *He was not one for small talk*
> *and, well, it seemed polite to go.*
> *I urged my horse around*
> *him   bluing with winter's fat,*
> *him   watching all the while*
> *nonchalant.*
> *Before my horse stepped off the rim*

he had taken back his bed.

Him   nearly indistinguishable
from the dusky rocks
and the liquid shade
beneath the rough barked juniper
yes, and the solitude of the rim
– the distance to anything
anything at all.

Every fall for five years I made that swing and every fall there he was, a little thicker in the shoulder and the haunch, antlers tipped heavier into the lower branches. The pungent tree combined his smell to make a bachelor feel at home. He watched me go my way trusting I meant no harm. I am sure he left his stand to join the does on Badger Mountain for the rut but, with that done, crossed the Flat where hunters wouldn't think to look, to the tree that spread above him through the seasons and held him braced against its circling trunk.

I think about him there looking down in his silent way, keeping track of how things pass by him and his silent friend, the tree.

I'm a tough, hard-boiled old cowhand
   with a weather-beaten hide
But herdin' cows is nothin'
   to teachin' dudes to ride.

I can stand their high-toned langwidge
   an' their hifalutin foods
But you can bet your bottom dollar
   I'm fed up on wranglin' dudes.

Anon.

Running the Lava Beds

After spring come Bud and Joe Richardson run thirty-five head of saddle horses into the Monte Cristo. They was part of the horses Bud fell heir to from out at Cow Creek, about fifty miles north of Lovelock, out there in the desert by Rabbit Hole. Bud wanted to go out for the rest of 'em so we threw our riggin's and some grub in this old Dodge screenside truck.

Ira took us out and 'course the girls, Jo and Phyllis, were with us. We were bouncin' along on this little old cow trail. Jo was sittin' in the middle on the gear shift and Ira was shiftin', first and second, first and second, and finally Jo growled, Hey! What's going on here? Ira just kept drivin', lookin' straight ahead. Business is business, he said.

It was way after dark when we got out to Cow Creek. A guy named Bob Knight, his wife, a boy, and a girl lived there. The girl was about nine years old, and I don't remember how old the boy was, but younger than the girl.

Bob had quite a little cavvy of his own, twenty or twenty-five head of good horses, thoroughbreds. Well broke, too. Mrs. Knight and the little girl rode 'em. The boy didn't do much buckarooin'. Anyway, we stayed there two weeks gathering horses. They had a corral in the field up next to the house. Just one corral. Then up the canyon about a mile was another corral.

We'd come afoot, without horses. Bob Knight loaned us one and Bud left one. We started runnin' horses with one saddle horse apiece. Whenever we corralled a bunch, if there was any that looked like they'd be good to ride, why, we'd lass 'em, and if they'd lead we'd put our saddle on 'em, and that's what we rode. We had to ride 'em right in that corral with all the other horses in there, but they was the gentlest boogers. All snaffle-bit horses. Heck, not many of 'em bucked. You could saddle 'em right up and we rode 'em, run horses on 'em. 'Course, we didn't have to shoe any of 'em – it was pretty sandy country. We were there a good two weeks. Boy, we worked, I'll tell ya. We'd run horses one day and then it seemed we had to fix fence the next. It was grueling. Geez! I lost a lot of weight and Bud did, too. We gathered sixty or seventy head.

One day we got a little brown stud. Wild, my gosh! That horse was as wild as any hawk you ever tried to catch. Bud got him to the corral down by the house, and he had a lot of rope, big rope. He tied it on that bugger and tied the other end around a great big clump of willows growin' in the meadow. Well, that bugger'd get scared and run and just flatten himself right out in the air. Bud left him there till by golly, he got used to things.

After we run so long, Ike come out and brought old Hicks out there.

That country was called the Lava Beds. How it ever got a name like that I'll never know 'cause there isn't any lava at all. It's all granite and right in the middle is the darndest country you ever seen. It sits all by itself. After you got into this lava bed country you couldn't see any place, all canyons or draws or peaks and pinnacles. None really high but high enough you couldn't see out. And a quite a few horses ran in that country. If you were on their trail, you just had to track 'em down. You couldn't just *run* horses, You had to study 'em and know the country.

Mrs. Bob Knight rode with us everyday. She was quite a buckaroo. And the little girl came along, too. She was only a kid, but she was a good one. Bob had gentle horses for her to ride and when he'd spot some horses he'd take her in a walk to get just as close as they could. I suppose he'd told her what to do, how to go with 'em. She had those good thoroughbred horses and just as soon as the wild ones started, she'd go too and you could see the space between her and the horses close up. She'd run right up on 'em. I'll never forget how she could turn those horses, get 'em goin' the way they wanted to take 'em. She was just a little girl on them big horses havin' the time of her life.

Another fellow came along there by the name of Ed Hardy. He was workin' for the Towells' outfit and had quit and musta been headed for Lovelock. He had a big, stout sorrel horse with a bald face when he come into Cow Creek. Bob asked him to stay on and run horses with us, and he helped us a little, but I guess he had other plans. He traded Bud out of two sorrel geldings out of the bunch. He stayed and halter-broke those two geldings there at camp, then he went on his way.

The last day we run horses we got a black-and-white pinto saddle horse. Gelding, he was. Big, tall rangy bugger. Pretty horse and a funny-marked sucker. Seemed like the black came down over his ears and across his forehead and he had glass eyes, or maybe just one. If he was off away from you, if he turned one side to you, you'd have thought he was a white horse, and turned around the other side, he was black. The black lapped over his back six or eight inches, but it was straight along his back. And his legs, the front right one was black, then the opposite hind one would be that way. He was pretty wild, I guess, and it took a little figurin' to get him in the corral.

Bud was finally satisfied that we had all of his horses. We planned to trail the bunch back to the Monte Cristo.

The day we left Bud was leadin' the pinto with his lass rope. He wasn't taking any chances on losin' him. He and Bob took the lead. Dad, Mrs. Knight, the little girl were in the back with me. When we got out of the field I noticed I hadn't seen Bud or Bob for a while. They'd been in the lead of the horses, but I thought I should have seen somebody. So I rode out on the side where I could see clear to the front and, by gosh, there wasn't a sign of a man anyplace. The darned horses were just goin' along on their own, so I got around to the lead of 'em. I knew somebody had to be up there. I had kind of an idea the way we were to go but not exactly. Hicks and Mrs. Knight and the little girl stayed behind. We traveled till almost noon before Bud caught up with us. That darned pinto horse had stepped over the rope and got away from Bud with that rope a-draggin'. Well, he and Bob had run that horse I don't know how far. Bob was still with him. Bud told me how to go with the horses as near as he could and said they'd catch us in the afternoon probably. He said he was goin' back and try to get that horse.

So we went on our way and, sure enough, they caught up with us in the afternoon and they had the horse, too. Bud said he stopped out on a hill and they eased up on each side of him and they had him. We were a couple of days goin' through the country. We came out of that big canyon on the east side of Winnemucca Lake and we crossed the lake and went straight through to the Monte Cristo.

When fall come I left the Monte Cristo with Dad Hicks for Duck Flat. I bought a blue roan horse from Bud that came out of those horses. He was branded with a †L. And I traded him out of a bay horse, too, an unbroke horse. The gray horse had been started, I think, but he'd shake ya. He taught me quite a bit about ridin'. The bay horse'd buck a little but he wasn't bad to buck. I started him. A'course, I didn't know anything about startin' a horse, but he turned out to be a good horse. I called him Stopper.

Business is business.

Flinty, lean, a self-contained man well over six feet, Dad Hicks was about sixty-eight when Lige met him in Reno during the 1927 Transcontinental Highway Exposition. Neill West had talked the old man into coming into town to add color to the exposition parade. Hicks was white headed and had a long white beard he cut once a year. His pale blue eyes were intense, alert to motives and dangers unknown to a milk-fed kid like Lige.

Dad carried around a violin in a flour sack and played it once in a while, not to entertain, just for himself. If he was outdoors he had a Colt .45 strapped around his baggy pants. He took it off indoors if he was with friends.

After the exposition, Dad stayed on at Bud Blundell's for the winter and helped Lige feed cattle. One morning Bud said he was riding over to West's. Hicks said he wanted to go along. Lige knew enough not to ask questions. He also knew Neill West had borrowed, for display at the exposition, an Indian basket made by the Washoe basketmaker Dat So La Lee. The basket belonged to Hicks's daughter. West hadn't returned the basket.

In fact, Mrs. West had the basket on a table in her front room. She kept it full of pictures, as if it belonged to 'em. Hicks said he was "gonna get it, and if they wouldn't hand it over, well . . ." He slid his hand onto the handle of the Colt and said he might have to take one of my horses.

He had a tall black horse he got from Bud he called Rudolph, and a bay horse he called Chip, branded with a flying U on the shoulder, but I guess he figured he might need one of mine if he had to leave the country in a hurry.

When Dad Hicks returned from West's with Bud that night, he had his daughter's Indian basket. The next morning he and Lige rolled their beds and left Blundell's ranch. They rode north to Duck Flat. Lige had it in his mind to stay at the home place and trap, maybe gather up any horses he and his Dad had missed in 1923.

During that winter on the Flat, Dad was sitting by the fire one evening, playin' his violin. He stopped playing and asked me if I could do something for him. I said I could. Dad pulled back the neck of his woolen union suit. There was an old wound, about two inches deep and big around as a fifty-caliber bullet, straight down through his shoulder. A scar puckered on his chest, like a sack top you might pull up and hand tie with a string. The wool from his underwear fuzzed and the lint irritated the tender skin in that hole. He asked me to take a matchstick and swab the lint out.

After that fracas in Beatty, when that guy shot him in the back, the wound wouldn't heal and began to smell bad, so Hicks said he poured raw iodine down through the hole. He didn't do it a second time. Once was enough. It finally got all right.

Hicks

Dad Hicks had a shadowed past, hard to track, but Lige remembered him talking about being a marshall in Beatty, Nevada, in the late 1800s. The isolated mining camp made a stab at law and order by hanging a star on a man who had experience with both sides of the law and was willing to be as bad as the bad men he was hired to keep in line.

Beatty was a hellhole for desert rats, miners, cowmen, and riffraff who loafed around the hard-bitten town. Makeshift saloons, fit with gambling tables, appeared overnight like the tailing piles on new claims.

On a winter afternoon Dad and two friends stepped into one of the saloons. Hicks was on the trail of a man accused of murder. Rumors connected the saloon owner to him in some other bad business, so Hicks warned his friends there might be trouble. The barroom fell silent as the lawman and his friends stepped up to the bar. Hicks told the bartender to pour them his "best whiskey, not that rotgut" he served the miners, or some such equally insulting description. The bartender took a bottle from a shelf and, watching them closely, brimmed the jiggers. Hicks asked the bartender if he knew the whereabouts of this certain guy. The bartender inched his hand toward a cocked revolver lying in the shadows on the back bar. One of men with Hicks took a drink and just as quickly spat it out on the floor, saying, "If that's your best whiskey I sure as hell don't want to taste your worst!" With that the revolver came off the bar and

Dad pulled his .45, fanning as he shot the bartender twice through the heart.

The room came alive. The lawmen were outnumbered. With their pistols drawn, they backed out the door. As they ran to their horses a rifle fired from an upstairs window. A bullet tore into Hicks' back, high up on his shoulder, angled down, and blew out his chest. Hicks was knocked into the horses and rolled under their feet as they plunged and pulled back against their bridle reins. One of the men dragged Hicks up and shoved him over a horse while the other shot into the upstairs and the barroom doorway to cover their escape. Hicks slumped in the saddle as they galloped away, his hands locked in the horse's mane.

He always packed a gun unless he was indoors with friends.

There Was Gold in Mexico

Lige listened to the stories Dad Hicks told after the whiskey was gone and the gray-bearded man forgot his vow never to speak of that time. He had gone across the border during the war and got run out. He wanted to go back. He *would* go back, someday. He sighed and in that silence after the words pulled the violin from the flour sack. It glowed with the glassy sheen of rawhide and cradled in amongst his beard like a dog turning in the weeds and lying down. He drew the horsehair bow across a string and a sound rose as clear and pure as a single star piercing the night sky. The held note blended on the next as one star belongs to a cluster of stars but, in its way, remains separate. Each time that first note was drawn again it shook in Lige's chest and made him want to weep. He turned his smooth face away from the old man as the sweetness of the music touched the place where all of his sorrows were kept. The music stopped.

Lige held his breath for as long as he could and let it run from him slow, holding that last sound inside him as if it was his father and, by holding it, his father would live again.

The old man said it was so hot in Mexico it sucked the coolness of his breath, the moisture in his eyes, as if a thirst bigger than his own moved across the sky and its tongue wiped the dust, the canyons, the arroyos for any trace of water. But the gold had him now. He stopped desiring women. His dreams were of gold. He tasted gold in every bite of food. Gold seeped around his teeth and filmed his throat until his stomach shriveled around his love of gold.

Following a map he carried next to his skin, he skirted military troops watching the border and traveled at night across the low country into the Sierra Madre. He had good luck finding the deep gorge penciled as a thin line on the brown paper. He pushed south until his burro fell from a rim in a rock slide. It struggled to stand but one leg swung in the sack of hide and hoof. He didn't hesitate but tumbled down through the rocks to the burro. The shot from his .45 echoed through the rocks and the silence after vibrated in his head.

Hicks butchered the burro, staked the hide to dry, stripped the stringy meat off the haunches, then battered the skull with rocks so no one would find the bullet hole and know there was a man in their mountains they should look for. Coyotes and birds would scatter the rest. Before the meat had a chance to cool out he threw some into a pan to fry and draped the rest on mesquite limbs near the small fire. The pungent smoke stung his eyes and he was suddenly absorbed by the joke. His laughter echoed against the rocks as the shot had done. He ate the burro. He would do the work of the burro. He *was* the burro now.

Hicks followed the creek downward working every cut bank and, one afternoon, was surprised to hear a dog barking and what sounded like children shouting in play. The next morning he discovered a poor village at the base of the mountains where a few families grew together like their corn rows beside the small stream of water. As the tall, white-bearded gringo walked into the square he pulled silence behind him. The villagers watched him buy coffee, drink one shot of mescal, and leave by the mountain trail. He returned week after week. In time the dogs forgot to bark when he came out of the canyon. The people forgot to laugh when he mixed their words with his own. Still, he was cautious, burying his pouch always in a different place so he would not be tracked. Standing before the storekeeper, he counted a few coins out, saving enough for one shot of mescal, which he carried to the coolness of the patio and sipped slowly, savoring its bite and the stir of people going about their work. When they had grown used to him, they spoke forth as if he was of no more concern than the magpies that fluttered up from the pig yard.

From the table in the shaded grove he saw the door of the church on the west side of the square open and a young priest dressed in a hooded robe carry his water jug to the fountain. The storekeeper called to his wife and together they watched the monk bend over the flowing pool. Hicks could not follow their quick conversation but their eyes were heavy on the priest's back. When the door of the small church closed it carried into the air a thick sound of timbers joining, and they listened, satisfied they heard the bolt set. The woman crossed herself and the man laughed at her and continued to laugh until she hurried off to the kitchen.

As June, July, August came and went, the storekeeper called out when the old man approached the cantina, poured his mescal, and set the lime slice running juice onto the bar. "Any luck?" he would ask, but the old man only took his glass to the patio and, as usual, ate the entire lime, even the hardest green nipple.

One evening when the priest came into the twilight with his jug the storekeeper carried a second drink to the old man in one hand, lime in the other, and leaned close to his ear.

> *The children looked over the walls of his garden.*
> *He laid out flat on the stone path. Rosary beads*
> *rattled through his fingers like castanets.*
> *He sang the psalms and wept.*

Just then the priest stood and turned his face to them as if the storekeeper had pelted him with pebbles. He lifted his arms out as a dark condor drying its wings at sunrise and, standing so, turned slowly in a circle. The sleeves of his robe hung away from his bare arms. A heavy wooden cross swayed in the folds of the frock. He stopped and looked at the old man. Agony writhed in his dark eyes. The jug sat under the spout, overflowing the rock edge and onto the sand.

Gold settled in the curved crease of the pan as Hicks spun the slur of sand and mud against the sunlight. His pouch weighed in his hand the size of a pullet egg and a year was gone. More frequently the old man found himself on the trail to the village without having decided to go. He began to understand more than the old couple's eyes and gestures. He realized he could understand even the woman who was no longer awkward with him near her. Some nights he took supper with them and slept on the bench beneath their oak tree but was far up the canyon before their white rooster crowed. Never again did they speak of the priest.

Hicks felt an uneasiness in the fall air coming up from the village. At first he couldn't grasp the change, and then it came to him. A foreign language was being spoken in the courtyard. English. He could smell the stranger standing on the porch in his baggy, soiled clothes talking to the storekeeper. The voice had the insistence of an educated man as he again pointed to the map spread across the table. Where the pale finger stopped his voice absorbed excitement but his body leaned away, detached.

The storekeeper saw Hicks and waved at him to come forward, saying in Spanish, "Tell this hombre if I hired myself out to guide him through the mountains, I wouldn't be here to sell you one glass of mescal a month." He reached behind the bar for the bottle of golden liquid. "Besides, I don't want to turn the soldiers against the village by going into their country. Let them stay on the mountain. Let them have all the gold they can steal."

The young man turned toward Hicks. His glasses swallowed his eyes and left only the black pupils. He smiled at Hicks the smile of the mouse a cat yearns for.

Hicks let the engineer follow him back to camp that night because he thought he might have food to share, and because the winds blowing down the arroyo woke him at night, and because just now he was lonely for home, and the words the young man spoke fell like a soft rain.

But coffee was all they shared. The anglo stored his supplies in a soft leather pack that strapped on his shoulders and fed himself carefully measured portions of tinned meat and tomatoes. He never said they should keep their things to themselves. He just did it, never offering, never asking for things that belonged to Hicks. By the firelight he lingered over his papers and maps, keeping records in a journal long after Hicks threw his blanket on the ground.

Hicks prospected by his senses, following seams up streambeds that broke open into glittering quartz deposits. The engineer looked for specific strata made up of combinations of compatible geology and made a record of ore sites he collected. To him, there was no such thing as luck. "Knowledge creates opportunity," he said, examining a specimen with his lens.

The year moved toward winter, the air cooled, and they worked through the day taking no siesta. The engineer pushed him higher up the mountain, farther from the village. Hicks decided to leave him on his own and work back down the drainages. The novelty of conversation became brittle. Their evenings lapsed into an uncomfortable silence, and Hicks was overdue for his glass of mescal. But his decision was one day too late.

As they prepared to leave camp at sunrise a line of dust came off the flat plain of the mountain directly toward them. Hicks knew it was no use to run and he took his .45 from its holster. The soldiers rode down through the rocks at them in a fan. Hicks stood in the clearing, his gun held steady on the leader. As the captain spoke, Hicks translated for the engineer. "He says they are hungry. They have had no food for two days. If we give them something to eat they will pay us in gold." He turned his head slightly so he could see both men. "I don't think they have any gold and I don't think we have a choice." He uncocked the gun and let it slide into the holster.

He watched the edge of their movements, their eyes passing glances as he scraped dirt and dark coals from a pot of beans buried in the ground. The men dipped handfuls of the beans, letting the red soup run onto their dirty uniforms. They pushed at each other for the last of it and licked their hands like dogs.

Hicks stepped back to separate himself from them and felt the captain's voice press into his back. "Why don't you and the young man accompany us to Mexico City. I would like to return your gracious hospitality." Hicks turned as the captain continued. "I insist."

They stood quietly as their hands were tied and ropes looped around their necks. They watched while the soldiers searched their packs. The engineer made no sound when his notes and maps were thrown into the fire and his ore samples dumped on the ground. The captain looked through the pile. "This is not gold. I thought you gringos only looked for gold. In Mexico City you will see gold."

The column traveled southeast all day, stopping only once for water. Hicks lost his hat in the morning and by nightfall he collapsed the moment the horses stopped. When they were untied the engineer carried Hicks to the shade, the old man weak with diarrhea and vomiting. The next morning the captain ordered two of his men to ride double and threw Hicks over the extra horse. Midday they came on a house and corrals in the bottom of a draw where two small creeks converged. An old woman wearing a black shawl over her head was working in a garden fenced by ocotillo. When they rode into the yard she yelled at them to keep their horses back and walked boldly to the man draped over the horse. "This man is nearly dead!" she spat at the captain. "What have you done to him?" Then she ordered the men to carry Hicks into her hut. Crouching beside the unconscious man on the floor, she dribbled water from a gourd into his parched mouth.

Just at dusk the music of muffled bells rang in the canyon.

Shortly after, a man driving sheep and goats came out of the twi-light. The woman went to open the gate for her husband and stood aside until all of the animals passed into the small brush corral. They spoke quickly by the gate and walked toward the soldiers together.

"What do you want of us?" he addressed himself to the cap-tain.

"A place to rest. A little food. No more. We'll leave in the morning."

"My wife says you brought an old man with you and that he's very sick." He nodded toward the house.

"He'll recover by tomorrow."

"And if he doesn't?"

"I'll decide tomorrow."

"Camp your men down by the creek and we'll prepare food, but you'll not kill that man as long as he's here."

"You're not loyal to the revolution?"

"I don't have to prove my loyalty to you, Captain. There've been other revolutions and I've killed many men. Maybe more, someday." His eyes burned into the officer's face.

The captain whirled and barked out at his men resting under the trees to see to their horses.

The old man went to the spring box built in the creek bank and lifted a hind quarter of goat meat to his shoulder. He carried it to the kitchen where the woman stirred her fire with small mesquite limbs. The fragrance of the meat cooking drew the sol-diers to her doorway and while they ate she made a broth for Hicks. Still he vomited uncontrollably into a slop jar she held for him. She broke herbs from bunches tied above the window and brewed a dark, cloudy tea. Lifting his head she pressed the spoon to his lips. He gagged and pushed her away, but she persisted until he held it down.

The sun broke through the cottonwoods that grew along the creeks and crawled across the floor toward Hicks. When its early heat touched his feet, a dream began.

He was standing with his face pressed against the garden wall of the village church. The top was high above his head. He looked closely at the adobe bricks. They were smooth, formed without hollows or cracks to let rain seep and rot. They would last forever. Forever. Not a word he had ever felt in his mouth. Forever.

Suddenly a chill centered in his spine, spread out his shoulders and up across his scalp. It swelled in him an urgency to look over the wall. At the same moment he was afraid to look. To see over the wall he had to step onto a large stone. He pulled himself up. The garden fell in a dark shadow of the church and he had to concentrate very hard to make out the smooth path that went from the arbor toward the heavy wooden doors. Slowly, his eyes moved toward the center of the patio to the body of a man laid out in a cross. His hands, held down by some unseen weight, pressed him against the blood-splattered sand. Hicks drew back as his eyes beheld the face, not of Christ, but of the anguished priest, a rosewood cross stabbed into his heart.

The captain kicked his bare foot.

Hicks struggled to open his eyes but the dream tangled around the captain's head. The next jolt was sharper.

Hicks pushed himself up and immediately vomit spewed

from his mouth. He spat into the jar. The bitterness of bile shook him. "Shoot me right here," he growled weakly at the man standing over him, "but I can't go on."

The captain's face grew dark. He turned and went out.

The woman came to Hicks with a cup of the tea that soothed him. As she helped him hold the cup she whispered, "You're his big prize. Two Americans to butcher for his junta will promote him. He wants you. If you are brave enough to refuse to go he'll be forced to leave you behind. My husband won't allow him to kill you here."

"I don't want them to hurt you people," Hicks growled.

"We're nothing to him. Now, drink this tea and you'll feel better, but don't let him see it."

The old woman was right. The captain shouted for his men to break camp. The old peasants stood gravely before the hut while the horses stirred dust in the yard. The captain rode his horse toward them but they stood their ground. He led the soldiers down the draw where they would meet the trail to Mexico City. Three men stayed behind. They led their horses back to the shade of the cottonwoods, removed the saddles, and unrolled their beds where they could watch the door.

Hicks was improved the next day but remembered what the woman said and gave no sign. As he made his way to the outhouse he stopped several times to bend over in the bushes, pretending to vomit. He did not have to fake weakness. The guards watched him from the shade and made sour faces but did not come near him.

On the third night the old woman spoke to him again as she held a bowl of soup under his chin and wiped drips from his beard. "My husband heard the soldiers talking tonight as he was coming from the corrals. They'll leave tomorrow and take you along, whether you die or not."

After supper Hicks asked the old man to move his pallet to the arbor so he could be near the outhouse. The diarrhea was gone but he pretended that it had returned, doubling over with a surge of cramps.

When the darkness settled Hicks staggered from his bed and fell headlong into the low bushes on the outhouse path. His moans were heard by the soldiers. The tall one crawled from his blanket and untied the engineer's ropes. "Go help the stinking old man. He's your friend, not mine," he spat.

The American looked at him, rubbing his wrists where the hemp rope left raw wounds, and then went toward Hicks. When Hicks saw they were alone he whispered, "Help me to the privy. We're gonna escape!"

Beyond the outhouse the two men pushed quickly into a dense thicket of mesquite and held quiet in the fear of the hunted. In a little while one of the soldiers called out. He called again. Then they heard him running toward the outhouse. In the light of the moon's thin crescent Hicks saw him stare into the open door. He yelled out and raced back to the others. The yard was suddenly alive with the men saddling horses. The tall one shouted orders as they rode off in three directions. The sounds of the horses' hooves faded into the high canyon.

The engineer started to climb out of the thicket but Hicks grabbed his arm. "Just sit tight. They'll be back." He released the young man's arm. "Thanks for helping me."

"You were going to die," the young man whispered.

"I would've if it hadn't been for the old people."

The soldiers rode back to the yard one by one. Again they searched near the house and corrals. The old man came out of the house and stood watching them. The tall soldier threw his bridle reins onto the ground and shouted into the old man's face, "Where did they go?"

"We know nothing."

The soldier raised his hand until the barrel of his gun was even with the old man's eyes. Hicks leaned forward into the brush. The dull click of a hammer cocked. The soldier's eyes snapped to the porch where the old woman stood in her night-dress and bare feet holding a rifle aimed at his head. She said nothing but walked forward until she could see the blood beating in his temple.

He lowered his gun and scooped his reins out of the dirt. He looked back again at the old couple before he swung into the saddle.

The soldiers took the trail north, away from Mexico City.

"Deserters!" the old man yelled after them. "Hah!"

She let the hammer kiss the firing pin. "My little Zapatista," he said, took the rifle from her hands, and left it beside the door where Hicks could find it. The lantern went out and the yard was quiet, except for the sweet ring of the goat's bell.

The two men traveled at night and stayed alive by stripping the skin of the cholla and chewing its soft, moist pulp. Hicks led the way down dry creek beds when he could, leaving no tracks to follow. They burrowed into the brush or crawled into caves or crevices to sleep during the day and hurried through the chilling darkness.

Hicks began to recognize the country. Two days later they

crossed into the deep arroyo where they had been captured. The engineer stopped where the path fell into the canyon. Hicks followed a deer trail into the bottom of the wash, drank from the pools a small family of peccaries had rooted in the mud, and climbed out the other side. The engineer nearly disappeared in the shadows. He was looking down where the canyon curved and dropped into the gorge.

"I'm going back. Finish my research."

"You're crazy. Them Red Flaggers will be after you."

The engineer shrugged. Hicks didn't wait for him to change his mind.

Hicks crawled out from the rock ledge and located the North Star in the darkening sky. He set out in the direction he felt was right. The trail narrowed along a rim and he pressed his shoulder into the rock face. As he neared the summit a scattering of rock echoed in the canyon. Hicks held his breath, listening for another sound. The rock could have rolled from under the foot of a deer, but a second sound – the click of a horse's hoof on stone – told him it was a man. Moonlight touched the end of his rifle and slid toward the sights, steady on the place where the man following him would appear.

The gleam of a bridle came in sight. Hicks recognized the rider's sharp face – one of the three soldiers guarding them the night they escaped. He pressed his cheek against the metal, cold turning hot. The bead laid in the notch sighted on the man's heart. A second horse came into sight, then a third. Hicks took the third first, then the second, and finally the first. The horses whirled, knocking rocks into the ravine as the bodies of the soldiers disappeared over the edge, then clattered back down the trail. Hicks turned back to the trail and hurried over the pass.

Two nights later he came upon a village. The smell of smoke and the wailing cries of women and children met him beyond the first broken fences. He crouched down and searched the square for soldiers. Women hunched over bodies sprawled in the dirt. Hoes and hammers lay in the dirt. No guns or rifles. Just then a deep hollow ringing of brass chimes bellowed out of the dusk. The glass face of a grandfather clock reflected the firelight of the burning church. The chimes were a confusion of noise. A man staggered forward with his arms stretched around the carved pillars of the case and, weeping, disappeared, the sound with him.

Beyond the village Hicks saw horses grazing along an arroyo. A brown gelding with saddle marks fed to the outside. He pulled the rope from his pants and ran his hand along the horse's neck. The rope, which had bound his wrists, was barely long enough to tie, so he stranded it and tied the ends to make a loop for the gelding's nose. He slipped a leg over its back. The last time he had ridden a horse he had been thrown over the saddle like a sack of salt, but this time he rode straight up and fast, crossing the border just before daybreak.

We trapped the Flat together the winter of '28, Dad Hicks and me. Hicks didn't know much about trappin' and I didn't know anything. The next spring his daughter and her husband came by. They was goin' up to Idaho to homestead. Hicks decided to go with them. I never heard from him for a year. Then he came through headin' south, toward the border. I didn't hear from him for another year and he was down on the Mexican border and he wanted me to send him some money. He wanted to come back. So I wrote him a letter with twelve dollars in it – all I had. A long time later the letter come back. I don't know if I got the address wrong or what. I wrote again but never heard another word. I always felt bad about that. I know he was countin' on me and I let him down.

On the Road toward Home

I sat on the hard truck seat beside my father watching where the headlights cleared the roadway ahead. Endless rain came at the windshield like long needles or comets. The mountain road blurred the radio into static. He had asked me to tell a story to keep him awake. I had no story ready for these long drives I could open up and read to him. I had weak copies of what I thought stories to be, taken from radio shows or something a teacher read in class. Dad listened to me for a while and then, keeping one hand on the wheel of where we were going, reached the other back into the satchel of memory – all the worn corners and rubbings of what he was.

He talked me to a place of real children born on a homestead beside the dangerous currents of the John Day River in eastern Oregon. His mother "whipped our bare legs with a willow switch all the way to the house if she caught us near that river without telling her first. It was the only way she could raise ten kids and keep us from drowning." By telling a story of himself as "just about your age" he was telling something about me. I felt the kinship.

Dad dealt no handset axiom: "If a job is worth doing, it's worth doing right." Instead, he launched the event that was on his mind at the moment. It was up to me to remember their two-story frame house that held its ground between river and rimrocks, the horse pasture a mile up river where he went every early morning to wrangle the horses home, to remember that

Grandma rode sidesaddle to her garden spot a mile down river, and while she and the four girls did the home chores, the older boys helped Grandpa freight goods to and from the little river towns of Kimberly and Monument to the Dalles on the Columbia River, or ran horses, or hired out to one of the bigger ranches during haying season. I had the sense from the first that each one pulled his weight. The little ones had little jobs and as they grew up more was expected of them.

His mother raised a little band of sheep from bummer lambs tramp sheepherders brought to her. Most of the herders were Irish and drawn to a country woman so like those they left behind or buried in Ireland. Moments in her kitchen, kids stirring currents of memory, her constant motion a tide touching home, gave them more than even trade for a wobbly lamb drawn from a flour sack slung over a shoulder. I remembered a photograph – Grandma with a herd of those lambs all around her skirts, bottle-feeding her "little toe-dancers" on extra milk until they were big enough to handle grass. Come fall she sold the wethers for cash and put the ewe lambs into the ranch flock. She raised livestock to feed her family, but something in the way her hand fell easily toward the lambs stuck in my mind.

In this story Dad was sent out to graze the sheep. It was an important job – coyote bitches were relentless hunters when they pupped in spring – but the sheep's pace was ponderously slow for a boy of ten. He threw rocks at the leaders to get them to bend uphill and wished for his father's dogs, Tip or Queen, to work the edges. At that moment the dogs were riding on the wagon with his father and his oldest brother, Ben, headed home from delivering a load of wool to the railhead at Heppner, and Dad was tending the sheep alone.

The ewes nipped tender grass along the rock ledges that held heat long after the sun went down. As they mowed up the steep sidehills, bells chiming in a nodding rhythm, he pitched rocks at coyotes he pretended were hiding in the brush. When they shaded up midday he also found a juniper or mahogany, pulled a book from his bag and a slab of bread flattened between the book and his sweating back, and read himself from the dullness of solitary hours into adventures with his chosen brothers: Tom and Huck.

On this day the ewes rose up, one by one, from the shade, heads low, and started to move. He cussed some words he'd heard Ben say and let them go out of sight before he closed the book and followed. That's when he saw the track – a ghostly brush of rounded toes and pad – on top those of the sheep. Puma. Cougar. Mountain lion. Panther. His neck hair took the chill on end. It nicked his gut. He dropped to his knees, hands one on each side, and leaned to smell the track. Pitch of scratching tree. Sage. Piss. Some blood. He rose up on his feet and laid his own bare foot inside. It took half his length and wider. He thought to gather up the sheep but then . . . A track was story to tell at supper, a track would capture the attention of his older brothers, but sighting the cat that made the track would be what Huck would do.

There was no plan to leave the sheep, Dad explained as he shifted the truck down for the grade, but each step took him farther away. He watched the thicker limbs and forks of trees because he'd read cats could climb and leaped down on the backs of horses, biting into their necks, clinging by the strength of their teeth and claws until the horse went down. Every sense tightened around the next track, twelve feet, twenty feet ahead.

The sun moved down the sky. At every clearing he stopped, held his fluttering breath, and searched the tapestry of broken woodland, waxy sheen of new leaves, dulled sunlight, for the autumn shade of cat that drew him deep in the broken country back of the rims where lodgepole pine grew into darkness overhead. Now the boy reached the furthest boundary of his bravery. He lifted his eyes from the ground. The sun swung from his shoulders and was suddenly in his eyes. The cat was doubling back. He turned and ran. Brush tore at him, rocks bruised his toughened feet, but he ran straight ahead, straining to hear the sheep's bells over his pounding heart.

The draw where he left the band was empty. Their tracks took him west to the spring box then cut back under the hill toward the old mine road. And then he found where the stampede started. It can be read, such a thing, out on the face of earth, where panic stays behind in chunks of sod and deep cuts of hooves. He searched till dark closed in and sent him home in misery.

His father waited at the pasture gate. The white of his bare forehead gleaming with moonlight, shirt sleeves rolled high on his arms. Tip and Queen wagged their tails at his approach. Seeing the sheep bedded down in the long lot by the barn did not console him.

"All but three," his father said into the boy's tear-streaked face. "Where did you see them last?"

"East of Gravely Creek," the boy got out.

"All right. Ma has supper waitin'."

"I'll go with you, Pa."

"You're give out, son. Go on in." He left my father guilt

enough to eat on for a week and started out, his sleek black dogs following into the night shadows of the canyon trail.

My father was to the yard before his head lifted from his chest. The cat. He forgot to tell about the cat and his father carried no rifle. There was no danger in the mountains like a cat. No one could fight a cat with empty hands.

He hurried to the house and pulled the screen door open just enough for him and not enough to stretch the spring and stepped inside. The supper table was wrapped in noise of passing plates and children's chatter. His mother's back was to him, spooning food into the twins tied with dishtowels in a corner chair. The rifle on its hooks above the icebox beside the kitchen door came down slowly to his arms. He took the shell pouch on his wrist and went back out the door as a fly might find a crack.

The rifle's weight cuffed against his knee as he ran down and up the pitch of the trail. The way to Gravely Creek was plain in his mind as in the moonlight. Then he saw his father's back, crouched down, the dogs and him. Ahead the fray of a sheep the cat killed and now, ripping, crushing bones, she ate it inside out. The dogs sensed him, then his father who quickly took the rifle from the boy and, broad hand to chest, pressed him back. The barrel steady before it bolted fire. The cat leaped and disappeared.

"My father was never a very good shot. Ben could always beat him at a target," he told me as he turned off the highway on our road. "Even I could, later on."

"The mountain lion got away?"

"Yes."

"But she killed the sheep?"

"Just the one. We found the others in the morning."

I wasn't sure if I should ask, but did. "Were you punished?"

"No. I didn't have to be."

My father stopped the story there. I watched his face in the dash-lights and saw the lesson lingered. I looked from his silence to seek the mountain cat that led a boy off his job, thinking it might appear in the long beams reaching down the road toward home, and saw beyond blood-pocked scraps of wool scattered in the brush a gift torn open, the wrappings blowing into me.

He fought his head like a bronco.

Old Mike White used to say a fella could see someone's dust on the road, walk down to the chicken house, kill a hen, and have 'er all fried up before the car pulled in the yard. That's how wide the valley ran.

The windmill stood mute at dawn. Lige climbed the tower, grease bucket on his arm. He painted the gears and snugged up the bolts while the giant slept. From that perch he could feel the distance of the Flat, to the smooth track disappearing over Mail Box Hill. When the sun tipped over Fox Mountain the warming air moved in the basin like broth being stirred. The slightest breeze slipped the fin to take it head on and the blades walked up the wind.

Lige prowled the country for the rest of the $\overline{\text{CF}}$ horses and one by one ran them into the pasture. It wasn't easy to do alone. He fought his head like a bronco being choked down but he learned as much as the horses did. His string wasn't fancy but they got broke, and he used them to gather more wild ones.

One winter when fur was high he trapped bobcats and coyotes. He lured them to the jaws of the iron trap buried in the dirt. He oiled the hinges, filed the giveaway spring to a finite snap. They didn't know what hit them unless it was a foot that hung, then they had hours to consider the error. They had a lifetime.

He brushed his tracks out, doused scent just at the trap's tongue. It wouldn't work without the fragrance of heat, bawdy piss laced with blood. Too naive to understand there are different kinds of traps, scent, bait, different kinds of hunters, he stepped deliberately into the cunning circle.

Francine came into the country with a woman called Ma Buckles. They lived on a back street in Cedarville, a clapboard house just around the corner from my folks' place, the French Hotel. You might say she hung out in the bar. That's where Lige met her. He had this thing about him. Always saw the best in a person. I guess he figured he could break Francine like he broke his horses but he never could teach her to ground-tie. Know what I mean?

Mike Semenario

On the Barn Floor

In the bottom of midnight the heifer began her lowing. She and the north wind moaned together. A stranger might have happened on us, drawn by the light at the barn door feathering out on the snow, cattle, horses resting in their shallow sleep, and thought it a refuge from the storm that wrangled the bare limbs of the cottonwoods and willows. But what we were doing inside was butchery. The heifer's body clutched the calf and would not give at the pelvis. Opening too small. Calf too big. We had tried everything and been at it way too long. With every heavy contraction the calf was being jammed against the brick wall of her pelvis. "Let's do a cesarean," I cried. John said it had gone too far. The calf was too stuck to attempt the C-section we'd watched performed in the Practical Ranch Medicine course a few months before. But in truth he was afraid of the first slash down a cow's stomach that begins the operation. There's no turning back, no throwing up your hands and going to the house. We bought the kit: instruments, surgical tray, antiseptic soap, topical deadener, suture by the bolt, antibiotic. All spanking new and not a speck of blood on any of it. I had my surgery notes handprinted neat as a bride's recipe folder. And he'd memorized all the reasons why we couldn't do it.

Early on, calving wasn't easy for me. I'd never been intimate enough with birth to know which hurt is reasonable, which is not. Running bulls with cows on the range creates a problem.

Bulls are present when early-maturing heifer calves, still on the cow, come into estrus. The heifer can get bred before she should, to a bull that's not genetically appropriate for first calving. Her body's resources are immediately diverted from her normal growth pattern to the budding fetus. Nine months down the line, probably in the middle of a blizzarding winter night, the heifer will pull off the feed ground, cast her tail stiffly, and snuff the frozen ground for a place to calve.

Nearly every ranch has a lot full of carefully chosen replacement heifers bred as long yearlings to bulls hand-picked for calving ease, small-boned, light birth weight, hopefully slim-headed. Even then there can be calving problems, and under the heading "best laid plans of mice and men," that middle of the night will come, there will have been a genetic backfire, and a calf that should have slipped from the vulva will lodge in the pelvis, too big, hind feet first, or have a leg back. The heifer will inch toward death if someone doesn't help her.

From the first winter of our marriage John and I took on the early spring job of calving our heifers. That's what we did – calved heifers, around the clock. For some a steady pull was enough, for others it was more serious. We did our best not to hurt them but sometimes we did. We culled our heifer calves down to 150 growthy Hereford/Angus cross heifers, eyeballed them for a decent slope from the hooks to the pins so the calf's presentation could follow the arch through the pelvis, and still there was trouble to tend.

There we are framed in the false warmth of light on hay, tired, frustrated, anguished. Again John fishes the calf's front legs out, pushes to his elbow beyond them, hoping to feel the pelvis give.

He works and works but there's barely room for the feet, let alone the head, shoulders, hips. Her body heaves with contractions. I feel her agony but only she knows the ripping pain. I want him to do *something*. I can't stand any more. John curses and hurls a bucket of water out of his way. He disappears into the night. He comes back with a hammer in his hand.

"If you're going to kill her, get a gun!"

"I'm not going to kill her, for Christ's sake!" He pulls a coal chisel out of his pocket.

"What's that for?"

"You said to do something. I'm going to split her pelvis."

"What?"

"You want me to take the calf out in pieces? Or alive?" he shouts.

"Are you serious?"

His grim face says he is.

I want no part of this, yet I'm unable to leave because I know he wants no part of it either.

We're opposite, the heifer between us. Her surging moves him. He hands me her tail. I grab it from him. His fingers locate the ridge on the lower plate of the pelvis, the seam that will not give. He lines the chisel and drives the hammer down like he's driving a nail through tin.

I turn away with a scream the barn door pulls from dry rails. I hear two more hard blows before the pelvis comes apart. He throws the tools, grabs the chains, lashes them around the legs, sits down behind her, feet braced above her hocks, pulls with his arms, pulls with his tired face. The calf comes fast in a gush of fluid and blood into his lap. He leaps up, clears the calf's swollen mouth of mucus, and drags it to the heifer's head. The cords rips. Blood spurts, then quiets. The heifer stares at nothing. John grabs the bottle from my hands, pumps colostrum till it foams at the cap, sticks the nipple in the calf's mouth. Its eyes suddenly alive. It sucks. Gurgles a weak bawl. The heifer looks around. Her moan is different now, to her baby. In minutes the calf staggers to its feet, falls flat, struggles to its feet again. Life, living, steadies it, holds it upright. The heifer stands, a hind hoof sliding braces against John's boot.

"I heard you could do it. Never did it myself," he said quietly.

"I hope you're not going to tell me, 'it's a long way from her heart.'"

"The calf will take her mind off the pain."

"How the hell's she going to get around?"

"I'll keep her inside, off the ice. Her muscles'll hold the bones together while she's on the mend. I know guys that split their pelvis riding buckin' horses. They limp around till they heal."

"They choose to do it. She didn't choose this."

"No," he says, kinder than I deserve. He sets a bucket of water down. While the heifer drinks he pulls out his knife, cuts her tail off below the bone to mark her for sale, and throws the hair down.

Between the barn and the house we don't touch. Drag off boots, dirty coats on the porch. The kitchen light shows us what we couldn't see in the half-light of the barn. A glass of brandy stirs the words we need to speak. Never again, we say. We'll try our best to keep this night from happening, but if it does we'll do the cesarean. No matter how it turns out, we'll try it. But it's not that simple. Silence rises up from the floor, cold, and holds him separate from me. Each seek support. He, the sink. I, the stove rail. The brandy burns. I choke. I begin to cry. John, the one needing to skin away a layer of himself, steps forward and takes on one of mine.

I wake at first light. John's side of the bed is empty. I go to the window, rub a hole in the frosty glaze. I can see him walking through the heifer pen. Some rise up, leaving smooth circular beds pressed in the snow. Some stop their chewing and watch him. They move aside. A black heifer, tail cast, hoof protruding, raises her head. I yank on my clothes and go to help.

C-Section: The Parting Line

You know. When you fit the chains around the tips of hooves, slick, slimy tissue torn where the hooves have presented themselves, made their entrance. Hooves first, like a diver except the dive carries this swimmer from the depths of pre-life darkness, dull senses through the passage – electric shock – to break the surface of light.

You know. When you with your pounds of strength pull against a thing as solid as the earth. Slap the rope around your body below the waist where the hips are solid and strong, twist the rope around itself below your knees, one, two, three, four, and lift! Can you lift the earth? It's the complete resistance that collapses your will within your brain and you know.

You could call the vet but he is miles away and we understand how time can steal a life as the rope unravels and the earth wins the pull. And what would we learn for ourselves, for the next time?

We gather the few necessary things – shining stainless tools that have a sacred feel in our hands, so near they are to the saving of lives. And thread. We'll need needles and strong thread.

The heifer is roped down. Legs tied like a tent tarp. Somehow she disappears behind us and her stomach becomes a bulge that is prepared quickly. I won't tell you all, it's too long, but now, the blade draws a parting line from which small rivulets run blood and it's on our hands. The thick wall of tough tissue, striffen, sinew that holds the weight of guts and calf is a wave, and through this opening I slide my hands. Do you understand? I reach inside these living waters.

I won't explain the heat and the pulse of organs because I must hurry – the calf – I must find the sack, the uterus and gently lift the weight of eighty pounds of calf and many pounds of fluid up where I can cut the thing that holds a life within a life.

One holds it. One opens it. The cut. Take care not to lose a drop of the torpid sea the calf is floating in. Eyes closed. Waiting.

One tries hard to hold it. The slick heavy tough thing that wants to leap like a fighting whale, pull away from the hand reaching in to find a leg, hind leg. The leg jerks back – Don't touch me! – and I can't help but smile.

Two legs up through this hole that opens on the sky. A third person is needed here to take the calf with block and tackle. Straight up! Carefully! Quickly! Straight up until the head clears! Cord taut, stretched, tearing like an air hose on a diver's mask might snag on rocks and tear apart.

Third person tends the calf, clears the nostrils, mouth of sludgey, rubbery fluid. The tapping within the ribs. The head shakes and this huge slick fish opens its eyes and breathes.

But we are with the cow, now. We two or three must hold the limp sack, hold the uterus up and quickly sew it, turning the edges in with the Lambert stitch, pulling tight so it will mend. So she can carry another calf in this stormy sea that held her swimmer safe through time.

Then the stomach lining. Then the skin and leave some space for draining. She is untied and rolled upright. The calf, her calf, is pulled to her head to remind her what this last forty minutes was all about. This calf too big to birth. Forty minutes to save one life, to make one life. And when she moos and licks the calf, I say a prayer of thanksgiving.

We wash up. We wash her blood and fluids off, unroll our sleeves, button the cuffs, unable to take our eyes away from the calf struggling wobbly wet to stand. He bawls. Her eyes brighten and she moos low and long. She gets to her feet. He staggers down her side, bumping her flank, ripening at her udder.

We go back to work. The work we were doing before we felt that pull, as if we were trying to pull the earth up between our feet.

Red at Red Rock

I brought two horses with me when Dad Hicks and I first went back to the Flat. One was a blue horse I had goin' good enough to ride outside. He'd shake the heck out of me once in a while just 'cause I didn't know how to keep him from it. The other was a good-movin' bay horse that I started after we got to the Flat. He was kind of a goosey bugger, a good mustangin' horse, still in the snaffle bit. Never did put him in the bridle, I don't think. I called him Stopper. After we got situated, I started ridin' around, lookin' for those $\overline{CF}$ horses of Pa's. There was a sorrel horse that run right close to home. I started him that first fall I was there. Red had a little age on him. I don't know how old but he was no spring chicken, by any means. He started good. A goin' machine, he was. Full of go but I lamed him some way. I did something wrong. The muscle all shrunk away on his shoulder and the cords stuck out under the skin. So I kept him in the field until somebody come along who'd know what it was. George Brooks and Bruce Marr stopped one day and stayed all night. First thing the next mornin' I went right out and got that horse to show them. Brooks said, "I think he's sweeneyed. I'm sure he is."

"What do you do for a sweeney?" I asked him.

"We'll tie him down and I'll show ya." So I caught him and did just what Brooks told me. The hide over the shoulder blade was just as tight as a drum. He started right at the high part of his withers and went clear down Red's shoulder, just grabbed the hide and pulled it up. Then he took a sharp knife and ran it right through the hide about every six or eight inches and worked the hide loose to let the air in. It wasn't very long and Red was all right.

I didn't need Red that fall, so I turned him out. I didn't get him in till the next summer. He got fat and that's where I made the mistake – turning him out, 'cause he wasn't broke yet. All he did was buck after that when I'd get on him. He wasn't bad to buck in between times, but he'd buck every time I got on him. That's what happened at Red Rock.

I was workin' for Lyle Cook, ridin' and stayin' at Red Rock. I was usin' some of my own horses. Lyle was a little short on horses, I guess. I was gonna go way off down to Cottonwood on this particular day, so I caught Red. It was a pretty long ride and he was tough. He could stand it.

I saddled him up. He was never bad to handle on the ground. Of course, he bucked when I got on in the corral, but I finally got him off the bed-ground. Down the road about a half a mile I come to the gate to get out of the field, so I opened the gate and led him outside. When I got on him again, that's where I had my wreck. I still don't know what happened.

Fred Mordy come along about noon the next day. He had been up at Clarks Valley helpin' Frank Ferguson and he stopped at the house on the way back by. When he felt the stove and it was cold, he started lookin' for me.

Red was outside the field, still saddled, of course. My hat was fifty feet away on the ground and my quirt was layin' out there on the ground, too. The gate was tore down and the pole that was the crossbar at the top of the gate was layin' on the ground and I was sittin' on top of it. It'd just rained and I'd been there all the day before, all night, until noon the next day when Fred found me.

Fred was ridin' this little savina horse he called Pinky. Gentle old guy. I remember when he rode up to me, just for a few seconds. He asked me, What are you doin'? or somethin' like that, and I don't remember what I said, so he asked me again and I gave him some two-bit answer. I don't remember anything that happened after that. Fred got me up, hauled me up behind him on Pinky, and took me to the house. Man! I was sure woozy. It had rained that night and I was pretty cold, so he built a fire in the stove and went to get Frank. It was about three miles over there.

Frank stayed with me while Fred rode eight miles over the top to Claud Davis's to get Claud's car. Fred and Frank got me in the car and headed for the hospital but they got stuck goin' down through Clarks Valley. Fred had to walk clear back up to Red Rock and get a team to pull the car out. Fred told me later I got out of the car and walked around tellin' them what to do about gettin' the car unstuck, a real authority, but I don't remember any of it.

It was plumb dark by the time they got me to the hospital in Alturas. I bet Fred and Frank didn't get home till midnight. It's about fifty miles back to Red Rock and the roads were pretty slick.

The first thing Doc Gibson did was look me all over, but only one thing showed up – my right elbow was as black as your hat. Other than that they didn't find another bump or bruise. They even drew fluid out of my spine, but there was nothin' in there that shouldn'ta been.

I only remember one thing happenin' in the hospital. A nurse walked into the room and spoke to me, took me by surprise like Fred did when he came up to me sittin' on the ground. I answered her. That's all I remember. Five or six days after that I finally come to. I laid there one whole day tryin' to figure out where I was and when I got that figured out, I worked on how I got into that place. When I finally come clear out of it Mom was sittin' by my bed.

Old Doc Gibson told Mom there wasn't anything he could do for me. He told her to take me home but not to let me do anything for a month. Just rest. So that's what I did. We got on the train for Reno and I was never so sick in my life. I threw up everything that was inside of me. God!

I caught a ride back to Alturas for the Fourth of July rodeo. They just drove up to the fence and I watched the show from the car. Lyle Cook was over there and he took me to their place in Surprise Valley. I stayed there one night and the next day I decided to go to Red Rock. Man! when I got there I was tired. I didn't give a whoop whether school kept or not. There were some Bascoes at camp tendin' sheep. I just sat down. I was all in. I wasn't worth a nickel for six months. Just couldn't stand anything.

I never did ride Red again. I took him over to Marr's and they sold him to a rodeo string at Susanville. They said I wasn't the only one he bucked off. He never failed to buck. He'd fire out of the chute every time. He was honest that way.

Bloodlines

Something woke me. It's still dark. I push the window higher and listen. Our stallion and the gray mare mix their music of deep drums and squealing horns. I know their song will end in the breeding. Yesterday he sensed the approach of her foaling heat and stayed beside her – two sides of a coin to be spent before dawn. Her sorrel foal, light-stepping away from the confusion, holds its head high in a kind of worry. Now the mare stands, the stallion rears up, gripping her flanks with his front legs. No need to see; sounds draw their own pictures. She submits because her body must keep working in this way. Between his peaks she snatches at grass absentmindedly and he prowls, his neck arched tight, smooth as a swan's. Every throb of his in step with her for a few days until the band that holds them tapers to a break. They have no friendship made of seasons. She arrived a week ago in a trailer and will be led from his pasture once she passes by her next cycle. Eleven months and eleven days is the country measurement of a mare's gestation, nearly a year for the birth of the foal he just began in her. Their finest traits combine, a dominance is decided and weakness pressed further to the shadows.

I learned the basics of genetics at our kitchen table. Before breeding season Mom and Dad got out the stud books and papers and developed a theory together. Generations linked backward through the stack of royal blue volumes narrowed to a handful of foundation sires. Their research, their treasure map of a blind journey, told me nothing was left to chance. Blood always mattered. An individual surfaced now and then but the odds were with blood.

What I heard, knew was happening just beyond the fence was not the summation, merely a step on the path. The test would come after birth. Their interest was in conformation but not just for conformation's sake. They wanted no hothouse beauty queen but an athletic horse, a working horse. "No leg, no horse" was an absolute truth Dad took possession of. If a sacrifice was made it was never in the direction of sound structure. Training provided another split chance for success or failure. But if a concentration of genetic power dominated, breeding would be proven in performance. It was a long-range plan, a devotion, carrying them toward something of value. This wasn't a horse to be roped out of a bunch. They made this horse to order and it was as scientific as a kitchen table, a stack of stud books, and common sense can get. Their deliberate concentration made me wonder at the value of my own pedigree. I was the obvious product of whimsy.

At the end of a rain-rutted road nearly overgrown by blackberry vines a small barnyard opened between a gray clapboard house and a small dairy barn. A dog waited by the gate. I waited in the truck. Dad never met a dog he couldn't charm. I didn't know what he said to them but they'd look up as if he poured food into their dish every morning and night. When he was in his seventies I saw him stand his ground as two Doberman guard dogs galloped at him, slobbering, growling, thrilled to finally have someone to kill and eat from hat to bootheels. He ignored their charge and kept walking, going on about his business. They followed him around on their tiptoes awhile, growling up at him until they lost interest and went back to their mats by the door. I was in the truck that time too, with the windows rolled up. It's a recessive gene.

Anyway, at that little forty-cow dairy, an old man came out the back door. I had a child's sense that he was born in the long dirty beard, rubber boots, and sloppy overalls, and that he couldn't take them off any more than his dog could shake out of its matted orange hair. He led us to the low, dark barn, took a halter off a nail by the door, and handed it to Dad. In the back of the barn in a double stall we could barely make out a white horse in the hock-high muck and long hay pulled from the feed trough. There were no windows on the back wall. The only life beyond her own was a flurry of pigeons coming and going through a narrow door in the upper story of the haymow. It was anybody's guess how long she'd been in there. Ammonia burned the air. Dad said if her hooves weren't rotted off, he'd shoe her. The old guy was busy kicking the door open and didn't hear him.

I led her to the creek and let the current wash her legs while Dad pushed his tools around the back of the truck, his anger escaping in a whistling that was no song at all but a mad noise of bees swarming. I held her halter rope and watched her look around. I think she'd forgotten what the sun was, and trees and grass, even. She jumped when a meadow lark flicked overhead and trembled when I brushed my hand down her neck. By the time Dad nailed on the shoes, he had her bought. He probably paid more than we could afford but he couldn't leave her in that nasty place. I led her down the lane. She pranced alongside me

like a butterfly. Dad tied her to a tree by the mail box and we
went home for the trailer.

While we were gone her ears grew a foot longer. Or else she
was a mule. Or else we were so upset at the condition of that
barn we didn't look at her very carefully. Dad swore to Mom the
old guy switched horses on him. It didn't matter. She walked
into the trailer, he closed the door, and we took Heidi home.

The next morning Dad saddled her up. He pulled his hat
down to the pegs of his ears and stepped aboard, ready for anything. He wasn't ready for Heidi. She untracked sweet as a kid's
horse, picked up both leads, switched on a figure eight without
missing a stride, stopped straight with that little *zzziiit* a stock
horse man hungers for. By this time he'd uncorked his hat and
was riding a Sunday morning smile. He asked her to turn. The
rein barely touched her neck. His leg fell lightly against her side.
She planted her pivot foot and came around like a top. Dad
pitched his hat over the apple tree and hollered this was his
lucky day.

Heidi was their show horse from then on, and until word got
around, the "white mule" was their sleeper. She wasn't pretty but
she won every stock horse class on the western Washington cir-
cuit that year. The next summer they decided to take her over
the mountains to the Eastern Washington Fair at Yakima. Mom
checked in at the office while Dad unloaded Heidi. He was saddling her when two other contestants rode by. "Hee-haw," one
brayed. "D'ya bring yer plow, farmer boy?" Dad smiled.

There were twenty-five entries in the championship stock
horses class. It was the toughest class Heidi had ever faced.
Horse after horse stepped from the line to perform the pattern
set by the judge. The pattern could be compared to the school

figures of ice skaters. Individual movements are those required to work cattle properly in a practical ranch situation. Each contestant is scored against an ideal of perfection. When it was Heidi's turn she did her work, balanced, fast, and graceful as a dance. She won first place. No one laughed when Dad picked up the trophy. No one could deny she was the best working horse they'd ever seen, big ears and all.

Heidi won every class Dad or Mom showed her in. She gave her best effort every time. Not because a pedigree predicted success. Not because she was grateful to us for getting her out of that horrible barn, away from that old man. Animals aren't capable of that kind of thinking, anyone who knows anything about science knows that. Heidi was an individual occurrence; a spark that would burn a theory to char. It was her bit of magic that gave me hope.

Part 3

. . . the second, when in the jaquima he
"asks for the bit" pulling on the jaquima
and foaming at the mouth . . .

*We come into Cedarville one night, nothin' doin' any-
where and we walked around town. We heard there was
a new church started up. One of them holy-roller outfits.
So we headed over that way to take it in. They were in
high gear, but they stopped their singin' and turned
around to see who we was stickin' our heads in the door
and motioned us in, real friendly. I guess they figured us
for a couple a slick-ears ready to be branded. The cow
boss started the song up again. Well, the music matched
up to a cowboy song we knew so that's what we sang —
"Roll On, Little Dogies," or one of those. I forget now.
Lige and me were gettin' up some steam singin' right out
when they all piped down and left us singin' solo. Heck
sakes, we never missed a beat. We finished 'er up, busted
out of their rodero, an' headed back to the desert!*

Buster Dollarhide, *buckaroo,*
Gerlach Land & Livestock

In my last year of high school I was called to the principal's office. There in the hallway stood Lige. I hadn't seen him, gosh! in ages. My first thought was Mom. I guess he could see that in my face and said, "I wondered if you'd stand up for me at my wedding. Francine's waiting out in the car." I didn't know who Francine was. I hardly knew him since he moved back to the Flat. I couldn't figure out why he wanted me, not Mom. But when he stuffed me in the car between him and Francine I could smell whiskey. Lige knew Mom wouldn't have gone for that.

We drove downtown to one of those little chapels on Fourth Street. When the minister asked for the ring Lige pulled a little velvet box out of his coat pocket. The ring wouldn't go on Francine's finger. Lige asked if she wanted him to spit on it.

I thought later the ring being too small was kind of a sign of their marriage. It didn't work out between them.

Margaret

Sometimes they danced.

Pearly Everlasting

The windows steamed with Francine's cleaning. She built a barricade of furniture outside the door in the snow and from the barn Lige could hear the door bang and bang as she carried buckets of water from the pump to scour herself into his life. She strung lines from rafter to rafter across the kitchen and washed all his clothes and starched even his work shirts, and made neat patches on worn places so you couldn't even see where the thread came through. She cut out recipes or invented them, substituting for items Maude McGuinnis didn't carry at the store at Sunkist, and she'd ask if he'd like this or that and he didn't even know what they were but he always said it sounded good. He gained ten pounds that winter on rolls and light bread and cakes. In the evening while he cut rawhide into long strings or mended his gear she read the paper to him or they listened to the radio. Sometimes they danced. One night she made taffy and they buttered up their hands and pulled it until it turned glassy. He kissed burned places on her arms where the boiling sugar popped, tasting the sugary butter slipping down her wrists. Ma Buckles and her husband drove down from Cedarville every week or so to play cards and visit and they always brought a pint of whiskey. The winter went by.

Lige worked his horses and hired out by the day to different ranchers. Come spring branding he stayed over at the Marrs' for better than two weeks and then Lyle Cook saw him on the road and asked him to help brand at Red Rock and then there was somebody else needing him. When he came home she had her dress form sitting at his end of the table. She kept talking to it even though he was there. He got mad and told her to cut it out and she threw a stick of wood at him.

It was not the miles of sagebrush between her and everything. It was not his hands that would be awkward now. He brushed past her on the porch. He'd take the first horse that came up from the meadow. He hoped it wasn't that damned mare.

Cotton print ran under the presser foot. Her foot on the wide iron treadle. The wheel turned. The needle pierced first the flat blue sky, traced the stem, inched up the wild rose. The tender grain of each serrated leaf laid aside for the sharp point, her foot rocking on the black pedal so wide she placed both feet together, knees brushing, pushing down before the rocking pressure returned like a piston's throw under her feet in a rhythm as the needle slowly plunged toward the rosebud pink as her bare toes hooked in the scrollwork. Down it stabbed through the double thickness, pushing threads aside, working toward the bud on the graceful stem, pulling ivory thread along, bobbin reeling in the hood, making chains above lock those below. The sharp needle stiched all the rosebuds to the endless sky.

Every afternoon he was gone she walked five miles across the Flat to have a beer with Maude and stayed till she could catch a ride home. Sometimes she didn't go home. He said he didn't like it and she tried not to go. She walked down to the windmill in the afternoons and watched the water gush up out of the dry ground to fill the tank, cupped it from the pipe to her face and throat. Sometimes she unbuttoned her dress and eased into its cool depth, lying out on the water, watching the blades slice the sky into equal parts. Beyond the corral the dark bulk of horses under the willows, side by side, worried flies from each other with a lazy swish of a tail. Those horses were Lige and the Marrs boys, never expecting, never asking, content to wait for the work that would come for them. She climbed the tower. The air took the water from her skin, bent the strands of her hair around her face. Then the tin roof blinked hot just at the base of Mail Box Hill. And even if she couldn't see it she knew Sunkist was there.

She opened the windows so air could move the silence around the small house. No screens. She searched the barn, the shed, climbed into the rafters. No screens. She pulled a dish towel off the line and stretched it over the window but that was worse than glass. Cotton muslin loomed tight to hold the silky slip of flour would not yield to light. The gauze square bellied in, surrounding her with its ghostly wave. She yanked it down. All the air of the world sucked into her deep vacuum.

Flies came in through the open window and touched their feet to her loneliness. Lige had made her a swatter from a scrap of boot top laced to a willow limb, three by four, small holes punched in even rows. Air could escape but not the fly. Limber leather. The handle end hit first, alerted the fly to an instant of calm – a splendor – before the final blow.

Lige and Francine lived at the folks' place on the Flat. I don't know too much about their marriage, really. Nate and I were in Petaluma takin' care of his folks' chicken ranch. It's funny to call it a ranch but that's what people said, "chicken ranch." Anyway, I think Francine was almost an alcoholic. She'd grown up that way. Always a good time for her around the bars. Lots of people. The Flat must've been pretty lonely for her. Lige was out ridin' all day long and she was stuck in that little house.

They took in two girls to raise. I don't know what happened with them but the next thing Mom heard they'd moved down to Gerlach. Lige was workin' in the gyp mine and Francine was runnin' a bar.

Jessie

The gyp mine started up in the early '20s. I worked loadin' buckets in the quarry all summer. Oscar Daniels used a well rig to drill the holes, packed 'em with black powder, and they'd shoot the wall down. Then I thought I wanted to do somethin' else so I got a job runnin' the jackhammer. Two of us. A little Eye-talian guy, Vince, and me.

They called Gerlach the Big Nasty. One guy said you'd see things there you'd never see anyplace else and I guess he was probably right. The Western Pacific was runnin' steady. Miners at Sulphur, Leadville, silver at Hardin, gyp at Empire, sheepherders, buckaroos all over the country, and they all came to Gerlach to let off steam.

Francine lay smooth as a pitcher of white enamel pearlized by the sun, turned to the wall counting twigs cast in the white-wash. He did not touch her but listened as if it was a love song.

Francine was the life of the party. She was treatin' all the guys to a dance. We was just havin' fun, all of us, when in come Lige, cold sober and mad as a hornet. He took hold of Francine and said it was time to go home. Well, she didn't want to go, and said so. Lige just lost his head. None of us ever seen him like that. He literally pitched Francine toward the door. She hit hard but she come right back and took a swing at him, cussin' a blue streak. It didn't faze him. He just shoved her out the door and then proceeded to throw her down the street. Every time she got up he threw her down in the snow again. She called him every name she could wrap her tongue around. He never said a word. Nobody stepped in. We knew better.

Mike

March 13, 1989

Out in the barn with a heifer on that night, John and I delved into a mystery – birthing a calf whose head lolled back once the feet broke the boundary of pre-life. John worked in that sightless place only the sense of touch can penetrate, slipping the snare behind the calf's ears and tightening the slide under its chin so the head could be held ready until a contraction could pop it through. I stood helpless, except to keep her tail from slapping him, feeling his agony as he strained to get the calf out alive.

We have developed a weird arrangement by which one wakes, dresses, and goes out to check the heifers while the other sleeps undisturbed. Sometimes the one getting back in bed will wake the other, who, in a dreamlike trance, fumbles out the door into footsteps that are still warm. But most of the time we take turns in a workable unscheduled routine. If there is a problem he/she wakes her/him, who stumbles along behind pulling on coat and gloves.

After the heifer and calf were saved from a fate worse than life, we went out into the corral on the east side of the barn for a quick check of the heavy bunch. The door opened onto a fiery sky raking the snowy peak of Mount Bidwell at the northern rim of the valley. I had read of the aurora borealis but had never been lucky enough to see it. The sky was opalized, alive, a shattered rainbow, beacons and floodlights. A carnival in the cosmos.

John remembered his mother taking him from his bed one winter night and holding him up to the window. As he spoke of it I imagined their faces, temple to temple, one small soft cheek against one smelling of cold cream she used as ritual to check the damage of the drying desert air – a woman pointing out the pulsing sky to a child too young to know what he was seeing but old enough to remember the moment.

On this night his cheek was warm on mine as we leaned against the feed bunk and watched solar particles dancing between magnetic poles on the arctic snows.

The Gerlach Land & Livestock Company

You'd ride up on some hill and wonder how far it was to another, and you'd look and it'd go on as far as you could see. No fences anyplace. All we'd do was pick out a certain piece of country and say we'd brand calves there.

Old Louie Gerlach formed the Gerlach Land & Livestock Company when he bought out Ward Brothers about the time I was born. When I went to work for 'em the spring of '29 Ed Waltz had leased the company from Louie's son, Fred, and O. D. Van Norman was cow boss. The company run fourteen thousand head of cattle and they entertained a dozen or so buckaroos the year round. Charlie Fuller, Jim Razer, and Ed Owens were cow bosses there before my time.

Van wasn't much of a cowboy. As far as roping goes, he couldn't drag a rope, really, but he knew cattle and how to run them on the desert. The cavvy always come first. If you had a sore on your horse, anything unusual, well, believe me, he noticed quick. He always kept the horses in fine shape. In the summertime he had that old Indian, Eddie, herd 'em outside on feed. At night they were broke to run with the bell mares. When I went to work for the company

Van had been there about a year. Before that he had his own place out in that Grass Valley country. He had raised horses and sold 'em to the company. That's how they got the Camp-stool iron. They used to brand with a TF connected but they quit using it 'cause it was too easy to work over, so they went to the TOL. They still had one mule in the outfit, old Stub, kind of a grullo pack mule that had the TF on him.

The ranch had been put together over the years: the Bare Ranch, the Murphy Place, the range up around Newland, Lost Creek on Duck Flat, all that country south to Gerlach, all the Buffalo Hills, all of Granite Mountain, and Squaw Valley, Clear Creek, Deep Hole, around Gerlach, then up the east side of Granite Mountain to Granite Creek, the Fly Ranch on the edge of the Black Rock Desert, Nigger Creek, Fox Mountain, Grass Valley, and the Hog Ranch. They even had cattle over on Donnelley Mountain. They had a regular ranch with a house, buildings, and corrals at Granite Creek and somebody stayed year round at the Fly Ranch and put up alfalfa hay.

Our winter work was to start the horses a-goin'. We stayed at Granite Creek. It was sandy country and you weren't apt to have a horse fall with you gettin' 'em started. The young horses had been turned out since they were marked and branded and they were kinda wild but that doesn't hurt 'em.

You get 'em gentle when you start 'em. We'd start about two dozen horses, usually four- or five-year-olds. They had to be old enough to take the long days. Van would split 'em up in the spring, a couple in each buckaroo's string, so they always had new horses comin' on. They could fit the day's work to 'em. Sometimes you'd get in a jackpot and have to use 'em a little bit hard, but that's just the way it was.

When I went to work for Van I was too young and I didn't know how to break a horse, the right way, I mean. I had started some, but I was kinda like old John Nelson. He said, "I can start 'em all right, but tell me, who's gonna stop 'em?" Later on I rode the rough string. Horses that had been started and turned out. Some of 'em were extra cranky and they were only payin' five dollars more a month to ride the rough stock. I squawked about that. Heck sakes, that wouldn't even pay for your riggin' that you'd tear up. I think they paid around sixty dollars for buckaroos and I made seventy-five dollars.

It was a good chance to give the young horses some easy days, get 'em started followin' cattle without askin' too much of 'em. We spent some time gettin' the cattle in order. We'd want to turn the dry cattle out first, so we'd get all them in a bunch, if we didn't already have them that way. When spring come we turned out the dries, then the cows with calves. There'd be calves to brand that were born in the winter but we didn't brand a lot of 'em inside on the ranch. We just turned 'em out. I liked that a lot better. You were bound to have early calvers. They was a lot of work when they got big but you could turn 'em out early with your dry cattle and brand 'em a little later on in the spring.

The ranch turned out the fifteenth of March or the first of April. Van had me stay out at Mike White's place a year or two in the spring to try and hold the cattle back from goin' up high on the mountain. 'Course they always wanted to go where you didn't want 'em, naturally. I'd stay out there for a month or six weeks and try to hold 'em down in the low country around Rye Patch and Duck Flat, then I moved the cattle up with the feed. But I had to be careful to move 'em off the rye grass so we could come back on it late in the year. That rye won't stand too much early pressure and if you took care of it by fall you couldn't see over the top of it a-horseback, and when the seed sets, the heads just drip honey. By the middle of June we started the calf rodero. You'd be surprised how those little characters grow if they have any feed to speak of. The cows that wintered outside would calve early and those calves are wild and big. Some of 'em get pretty woolly.

One year we were brandin' calves at Lost Creek and Ed Owens happened to come up there in a car. Of course, I'd heard about him. He was a hell of a roper in his day, I guess. Van got him on a horse and I thought, Now I'll get to see him rope. He used a loop that was about as big as a barn. Man! A monstrous thing! This little calf was a-trottin' across the corral and he just slid that big loop out there. The calf run through it, see. How he got all that rope gathered up and coiled up, I'll never know, but he had that calf by both hind feet. Those old riata guys, that was the way they roped. Buze Miller was one, and the Tahams, Mole and Jim. I guess Jim was the better roper, but Mole was good too. You know, catch a hundred and forty calves and never miss a loop. They all used riatas. There weren't any nylon ropes in those days, of course. Hemps and maguey was so stiff you could climb up one and it wouldn't even bend. There was always somebody buildin' a riata in the bunkhouse at night. That's where I learned to braid.

Anyway, I was tellin' you about the spring brandin'. We'd make a circle clear around the range. It'd take us about six weeks or two months to finish. Then the cattle are on the range for the rest of the season, so it'd take somebody to keep an eye on 'em, keep 'em salted, and check the water-holes so they got good water. Just take care of 'em.

Van wasn't just a boss. He worked right alongside the men, always, and he was heck for improvin' the range. One year we'd been up in the Granites and stayed at Stockade all summer. It was dry and not a good year. All we did was dig waterholes. Van had the chuckwagon mules and an extra team or two of mules and we had some wheel scrapers, so we stayed right there at Stockade and built reservoirs and fixed springs. Up above Stockade was a spring called Three Troughs that ran about enough water for two calves and a rabbit. Grass everywhere but no water. Van knew where this spring used to be before it quit runnin', so he took the crew up there and they started diggin'. He'd sent me off somewhere to do somethin' else and when I got back they'd dug out that spring and put the water into a trough. They had water enough for three hundred head of cattle! You just wouldn't believe it. Same thing in the Buffalo Hills. We scattered cattle around everywhere.

When it come to hayin' time those that weren't needed to ride helped with the hayin'. 'Course that'd take a couple months and then it'd be time to gather beef: the cows or steers they wanted to sell. So we got to ride all the range again to gather them.

One spring looked to be a good grass year, so Waltz went off to Idaho and bought three hundred head of two-year-old steers. Big wallopers. We didn't have to scatter 'em. They scattered themselves. 'Course they didn't know the country and they went in every direction. That was the last time Waltz did that. When he wanted to sell 'em we rode and rode and rode. It seemed like we rode all summer and fall. We saw the country that year, I'll tell you. The ones we found were big and fat, but I don't think we ever did get 'em all.

In the fall we'd gather the cattle and work 'em, get 'em ready for winter. We didn't usually start feedin' hay until around Christmastime, so while we classed the cattle, we held the cows on the meadows. We weaned the big calves and as quick as the cows dried up they were ready to go back to the desert for the winter. They'd be in good shape and in the spring they'd come with the feed. Those cows would be so much stronger than the cows with calves we kept in and fed hay to. 'Course they had a calf pullin' 'em down, but still, the cows that ranged out on that low desert country wintered just fine, out rustlin' instead of waitin' for the feed wagon. We kept the small pairs in on feed, to keep the cows producin' good milk.

There was a bad drought in the '30s and we run out of hay the first of January. The company was running about seven thousand head of cows then, so we went through 'em and pulled out about two thousand head of big fat drys that could stand to rustle a little. We drove 'em down to the desert and I fed cottonseed cake all winter. I don't think we lost a half a dozen cows. I didn't have to hunt 'em up once they got a taste of the cottonseed. They'd come a-runnin' to the pack horse.

They'd sent up a little mare from down below. The cowboys'd been trying to ride her but they didn't have any luck so they sent her up to us. Van gave her to Red. Gosh, she was nice to handle on the ground, but Red got on her in that long corral and I think he made one complete circle, then she jumped out, settled down about two feet, sucked 'er back, and just laid Red right out on his back. Didn't hurt him, but his spurs just came down and drove into the dirt! Jiminney Christmas! By that time the dinner bell rang so we went to the house to eat. After dinner I went one way and Red and somebody else went another way. He said she bucked him off the same way that afternoon, just like she did in the corral.

So then Van gave her to me to pack. I put two sacks of cottonseed on her. I just laid them on top of the pack saddle and tied it down with a rope 'cause I'd just be takin' it off, the first bunch of cows I come to. The horse I was ridin' was just a snaffle bit horse. Well, the first big brush I rode by dragged up the side of the alforkses and man! I looked back and the air was full of cottonseed cake! It was flyin' and that little horse I was ridin' wasn't stickin' around. He was a-leavin'! I got just one turn on my lead rope before she hit the end. It jerked her head up and she run right up the rope and hit my horse in the hind end. When she hit him he bogged his head and bucked me off. I hit right on the flat of my back, just like Red. I lost the mare but I hung onto a rein so I had my saddle horse. I got up but I didn't remember anything. I don't even know how I got back to the house. I was knocked out the rest of the day.

One thing about Waltz, he always hired good cooks. Van insisted on it. He said you couldn't keep good men otherwise. The company ran one wagon and it went everywhere we were ridin'. Of course, they carried our beds, all the food, everything we needed. They had four mules, Jack, Pet, Bird, and Cotton, on the chuckwagon. Jack and Pet were the wheelers, Bird and Cotton were the leaders. Cotton was a black mule with a big white nose. Bird was a bay mule. Pet was a big white gentle mare mule, and Jack was a black horse mule. There wasn't much Van didn't know about workin' those mules. We was there at Buffalo one year and they had a big fruit orchard behind one of the houses. Some of the trees had died and we were draggin' 'em over to the woodpile. Van had Pet and Jack draggin' those trees. Maybe he'd have a pretty good pull and I seen him take the end of his lines and whip 'em right down on the hind legs, way down above their foot, just a little bit before he started 'em, and boy, I'll tell you, they'd get in the riggin' now. Whatever he had to pull, they'd get it.

Once in a while a cook would get cranky, but we'd joke 'em along and they'd either soften up or quit. A big Dutchman, Joe Snotherly, cooked for a while. He was a real cook, too. We branded calves one day and he liked to rope, so he helped us. After we finished he went outside the corral and sat down on the ground, and that was it. He died right there at Stockade.

After that the Gopher cooked on the wagon for Waltz. I got acquainted with him over at Marr's. It was them that hung the name "the Gopher" on him. His real name was Fred Wright, but "the Gopher" was all we knew him by for years. How he got up in that country, I'll never know. Just showed up. He was a little guy, no bigger'n a bar of soap, and a wise little character with great big ears that stuck right out, just kinda hung out there. And he had a kind of a hump up between his shoulders. He was about as wise as he looked, too. He could do any darned thing. If there was something special that sounded good to eat, you could just brag him up and tell him you heard he was a good cook at makin' that and he'd have somethin' like it brewed up the next day. You could count on the Gopher to make 'er western. He'd come into the Bare Ranch with those mules runnin' flat out, right down through the yard, and everybody better get back! Really whoopin' 'em up. And he could do the hula, too. Get up on the table and why! he'd put them hula girls to shame! The Gopher, he was quite a guy.

Ormus Nay cooked one year when we were camped at Grass Valley. He and Van had a runnin' discussion, I guess you could call it. Not really a fight. It was worth gettin' up in the morning just to hear what those two would come up with. Before breakfast there'd be something wrong with one or both of 'em, and they'd go to talkin'. Van had borrowed Buck, Nay's big old potbellied horse. Why, he couldn't out-run a duck. Nay give him to Van to corral some horses and I guess Van lost the horses because he couldn't head 'em off on old Buck. Old Nay said, "If you'd just let him out!" And Van spouted, "Let him out? I did everything but take off the bridle!"

One spring an old fella showed up at the ranch. He'd been a judge somewhere sometime, and so he took on the job of cookin' for Van. I think he was an old friend of Waltz. Seems like I remember that he came up to this country for his health. One night at the ranch he had a few drinks and got tapped off about right and he preached a whole sermon on one verse of the Bible. He had a lot of these modern preachers skinned a mile

The summer he was there we were out at the Fly Ranch hayin'. Been there the whole blamed summer. Never left, never went to town. We finally got the hayin' all done and the crew made some reason why they had to go to town. They all piled in this old truck and headed for Gerlach. I don't remember why I wasn't with 'em, but Van was. Well, they kinda got bogged down at one of the bars and it was late in the afternoon when they got back to the ranch. Waltz and the judge was there when they drove in. They had got a flat tire someplace, but Van didn't notice it and he'd been drivin' on it for quite a ways. In fact, the tire was just a few strings draggin' behind the rim.

Well, Waltz was always a pretty serious man, didn't go in for any foolin' around, and he was mad. Said he was gonna "fire the whole bunch, startin' with Van!" An' he said, "Somebody better fix that tire!"

None of 'em was navigatin' too good, but they knew they was in trouble so they tried to be serious. They got to laughin' and wrestlin' and rollin' around in the dirt. Waltz was gettin' madder. The judge took Waltz into the house, the boys packed Van to the bunkhouse. I was the only one sober enough to fix the tire.

The judge musta used all his preachin' talent with Waltz, 'cause after a while Waltz came out of the house and walked over to the bunkhouse. He woke Van up for supper and he never said another word about the firin' thing.

Van knew cattle and how to run them on the desert.

O. D. (Otto Daniel) Van Norman, 1876-1981

█n the late 1970s the Modoc County Historical Society started collecting oral histories, and I was sent to Warnerview Rest Home with their tape recorder to interview O. D. Van Norman. I had secret hopes of finding, like Thomas Berger, my Little Big Man in the quiet face that regarded me from a chair by the window. O. D. Van Norman had been described as the last survivor of the 1911 Little High Rock Canyon Massacre Posse. That's the story I was prepared to take away for posterity in the black plastic case.

Four Prominent Sheepmen Shot By Cattle Rustlers

The New Era, Alturas, California

February 15, 1911

One of the most cold blooded and brutal murders known in modern history has just come to light during the past week, the victims being four prominent stockmen well known in Modoc County. Harry Cambron, and Peter Erramouspe of Eagleville, John Laxague and Mr. Indiano, a Frenchman. Each of the men had been killed by being shot in the head. Their bodies, stripped of their clothing, were piled up in a heap.

Four accounts have been published to date of the massacre of four Surprise Valley stockmen in the wintry Little High Rock Canyon of Nevada, and each one figures the facts differently. Despite their differences, all four versions agree on these facts: a posse was formed from the ranks of the settlers after a search party returned to Eagleville from the desert "out east" with a grisly account of the murder and mutilation. Frozen tracks at the death scene implicated Shoshone Mike and his family. They had been seen camped in Little High Rock Canyon: three men, three women, a girl, and three small children. The posse set out moving fast to make up Mike's nearly two-week head start, tracking them across Nevada through the worst kind of weather to the battle in a brushy draw north of Winnemucca where they ran the Indians down, and death was there, too.

High Rock Murders May Have Been Indians

Posse Close on Trail & Fight Hourly Expected

The New Era, Alturas, California

February 22, 1911

Ten well-armed men started out of Eagleville the morning of February 8th, nearly 20 days after the last time in which the missing men were seen following what they believe to be the plain trail of the criminals through the wilds of northern Nevada. It is thought that the crime was committed by a band of Indians, the tracks showing seven men, one mahala and three children to be in the party.

O. D. Van Norman was used to strangers appearing in his line of vision with pills in pleated paper cups, so he looked on kindly while I pulled a chair across from his. He was a handsome, sturdy man even in his advanced years. His were work hands, squared up and large, folded gracefully in his lap. He rarely talked of the massacre, but as the other members of the posse died, he was singled out to repeat the story until it struck into his mind like a shaft of light and he was illuminated with the remembering.

CHASE ENDS

Twelve Indian Murderers Overtaken by Officers and Engage in Desperate Battle

The New Era, Alturas, California
March 1, 1911

On Sunday at dawn the outlaws were finally surrounded and a desperate fight had near Rabbit Springs 25 miles northeast of Golconda, Nevada. The battle lasted about three hours, with the result that eight Indians were killed, four captured, and one white man killed, Ed Hogle, of Eagleville.

The Indians are Shoshone or Snake, and are a renegade band from the reservation in the Owyhee country in Idaho. It is certain they are the murderers of the four stockmen, as the trailers found several fragments of clothing taken from the murdered men.

He began in a strained, high-pitched voice as if it was once again February 8, 1911, and the search party had just reached Billy and Mattie Denio's cabin on the flat five miles west of Little High Rock Canyon. The tired men grouped around the young couple, listening to every detail of their evening of January 17, imagining the slip of Indians along the rims that had frightened Mattie weeks before, feeling the air for an idea of where to look for the four livestock men gone missing.

The New Era, Alturas, California

March 15, 1911

The chief of the band was Old Shoshone Mike. The remainder were his sons and their families. It was really a renegade family who escaped from the reservation in Idaho and have been roaming about for years living on what they could kill or steal. Old Mike lived for about two hours and confessed to the murders of two other men.

Harry Cambron, overseer of the Humphry-Moffat cattle that ranged into the Little High Rock country, was of particular interest to Mattie. He had not returned to Eagleville for his wedding to Mattie's sister, Laura Murphy. Cambron was last seen with Surprise Valley sheepmen John Laxague and Pete Erramouspe, both married men with children, and Bert Indiano, their herder.

Indiano met up with the three other men at the Denio cabin on the afternoon of January 17, 1911. While Mattie fixed supper he told them he had come on the butchered carcass of a beef in Little High Rock Canyon. Cambron, Laxague, and Erramospe insisted he take them there in the morning. Long before the sun crossed the rim of the canyon the four men rode east from the cabin, the horses' hooves barely tracking the frozen snow. It was the last time they were seen alive. Their disappearance carried a sense of foreboding. They all knew the country intimately. They all knew how to survive even in this winter, the worst in memory. But it was ludicrous to think they were holed up somewhere in the desert for three weeks, leaving Laura waiting at the church for Harry.

> The squaws fought with guns and bows and arrows, while the bucks had high power rifles, besides the weapons they had taken from the murdered men. The fight lasted as long as any Indians who could fight were alive. All that survived was a 16-year old girl and three small children.

The Denios got word into Eagleville and a search party was formed immediately. The men, including thirty-year-old O. D. Van Norman, rode through belly-deep snow drifts to the Denio cabin. Mattie told them Indiano was uneasy about going back into the canyon, that he protested the idea of returning, saying he had seen smoke rising against the dark rocks and was sure Indians were watching him from the willow thickets. Mattie said Indians had been coming near the house in the last few weeks but never bothered her so she put it out of her mind. In the end the others convinced Indiano to lead them to the dead beef.

> The youngsters fought like wild cats when captured, and one boy, aged eight, when he found he could not escape tried to kill himself by bashing his head on the horn of the saddle after being tied on to a horse. The girl fought so fierce that it took two men to hold her.

The search party split up and rode slowly away from the cabin looking for any sign at all to follow. In the mouth of Little High Rock Canyon, where the deep gorge splits open, Warren Fruits of Eagleville spotted something red beyond the willows. He got off his horse and tugged at a bandanna. It was tied solid to something beneath the snow. A deeper chill than the freezing storm must have passed through him. He dug down, dreading what he was sure to find, mutilated bodies of four men frozen together, piled over with brush and snow.

> Effects found by the posse in the camp of the Indians showed conclusively that the band had returned to the wild state of Indians whites fought in the State's earliest days. Bows and arrow, war spears and tomahawks, two Indian war drums, and a war bonnet of feathers, probably the headdress of Old Shoshone Mike. They were real savages, of unmixed blood.

Photographs taken February 13–16 by G. L. Mathews of Cedarville were published in the *Humboldt Star*. Plate 1 pictured a deserted willow-braced shelter in the rims near a rock barrier built to hold horses. The camp was a short distance from the bodies of the men. Plate 2 is of gaping canyon walls and a double scene of butchery, beef in the center, men in the south drainage. Plate 4 shows frozen bodies partially covered with snow, legs and arms tangled. In plate 3 the men have been pried free from each other and placed on stretchers to be carried $1\frac{1}{2}$ miles to a waiting sleigh. The bodies were then taken to the Denio cabin for the inquest in plate 5. Plate 6 gathers Captain

Donnelley and the twenty-three-member posse in front of the cabin with pack animals and dogs. As the men endured the ten-day ordeal on the trail of Shoshone Mike's band, the bodies thawed in the Eagleville church. Their bloodstains were visible in the hardwood floor for decades.

The front page of the Reno Evening Gazette, February 26, 1911, reported the proceedings of the inquest and listed the Indians killed at Rabbit Creek, with their ages:

Squaw Jennie	40
unknown boy	10
Shoshone Mike	55
Buck Disendy	18
Buck Kennan	23
Buck Cupena	25
unknown squaw	17
unknown boy	12

Possessions of the Indians recovered: five arrows, drum with two bullet holes, spear made out of old butcher knife with willow handle wrapped in red flannel.

Surviving Children:

Squaw Snake	15
Squaw Heney	17
boy	5
girl	infant

Credit For the Posse

The New Era, Alturas, California

March 1, 1911

Captain Donnelley and his men began at the beginning and remained to the end. They did not speculate. They did not falter. Without haste and without rest they followed the trail. When the grinding monotony of the pursuit changed to the fierce activity of warfare, they were equal to that emergency and throughout it all they comported themselves with credit and honor to the best traditions of the race.

After he described the chase in extreme cold, jaded horses, and worn men driven by their sense of justice to the brutality at Rabbit Creek Wash, O. D. Van Norman fell into silence. The machine turned but no words tracked the tape. I was no longer in the chair across from him. I had disappeared into the glare of snow, the pinching smell of gunpowder, my voice layered beneath the cries of the survivors of Shoshone Mike's band: Hattie, Cleve, a baby, and a brave girl named Heney.

O. D. Van Norman had been given a second description by the people who sent me out, as an "old cowboy." I went back a few times to ask more about his life, and he would begin at the age of ten when he came onto the back porch and overheard his parents in a row. They were dividing up the marriage and the children. He said he didn't intend to stay around to be bounty or bait, so he set out on his own with a saddle horse and the clothes he had on. Then, as if the needle jumped across the grooved years, he slipped into the story of the massacre and nothing could stop him or bring him back.

It was later I learned from Lige that Van was not just an "old cowboy" but the cow boss for the Gerlach Ranch, one of the largest in the country, that he had the responsibility of cattle, men, and horses in a harsh and wild country, that he gave more orders than he took, that he made mistakes, and that he enjoyed the respect of other livestockmen. O. D. Van Norman had witnessed a drama of history and lived more than one hundred years. He was a man I would never know. To hear the days of his life, to really hear, I was too late.

Humboldt Native Dies, The Last Survivor of Shoshone Massacre

March 26, 1993

Humboldt Sun, Winnemucca, Nevada

The death of a Humboldt County native – the last known survivor of the 1911 Shoshone Mike Massacre – has been attributed to being given the wrong medication at a nursing home.

Mary Jo Estep, 82, died Dec. 19 at Good Samaritan Health Care Center in Yakima, Wash. At least three investigations are under way into her death, as she received no treatment after staff at the center realized the error.

Estep was a member of the Shoshone Mike band of Bannock Indians, who refused to give up their nomadic ways and settle on a reservation. In 1911, her parents, grandparents, aunt and uncles died in a confrontation with a 20-man posse north of Golconda.

Four children survived the three hour battle, but all but Estep died of tuberculosis within a year. She was raised by whites and became an elementary school teacher.

The Social and Health Services report says Estep was accidentally given three doses of medication intended for another resident.

The mistake was discovered within a half-hour, but no corrective measures were taken because Estep had signed a directive barring extraordinary measures to keep her alive. A nurse who had power of attorney in Estep's health matters called the woman's physician, but he refused to take the call. Shortly after that the nurse declined the center's offer to rush Estep to a hospital. She died shortly before midnight.

The Shoshone Mike Massacre, as the incident is known, occurred Feb. 26, 1911, and is the last recorded Indian massacre in the United States.

The small band was accused of killing a cattleman and three Basque sheepherders and its members were pursued from the western edge of the Black Rock Desert to Rabbit Creek north of Golconda – a distance of 200 miles – where they were killed.

I can remember very plain, when the haying was over, Dad would go up to the bank in Cedarville and get three or four alfalfa seed sacks full of money — bills. Then when the Indians left to go back to the reservation, they would come into the office and Dad would ask, "How many days did you work?" They'd say a hundred or fifty days, he'd roll out the greenbacks to them, and away they went with no bookkeeping or nothing. He allowed Indians who retired from Gerlach Livestock Company to live on the ranches, acting as caretakers. He was fired for it. My brother and I went out to visit him and he was loading his saddle and bridle into the old Model T Ford pickup. I asked him what he was doing and Dad said, "Well, this guy says I got to take the Indians off the ranches and send them back to the reservation. I told him if one Indian left one of the ranches, I'd leave with them." After thirty-seven years with Gerlach Livestock Company all that he had was in the back of that old Ford pickup. We didn't know what to say.

Philip Van Norman

The Blood Bay

I rode in the lead of the bunch. The pretty bay horse got right behind me, like I was leadin' him. Just stayed right there. Man, he was a pretty sucker.

Van Norman claimed all the horses that ran in the Buffalo Hills for the company. There were hundreds of horses and they didn't all belong to the Bare Ranch, by any means. Buffalo Meadows had WS- horses. The Marr boys had horses that ran into that country, maybe stayed there. My dad had the $\overline{CF}$ horses. Van decided to gather what he could and clean out the Buffalo Hills.

I ran onto three geldings all in a bunch. All bays. Good lookin', they was, and gentle. You could handle 'em, drive 'em. Anybody could, if you knew anything about horses. One of 'em was a big tall rough horse. Looked like he'd be a good mustangin' horse. There was a bright red bay horse, a blood bay, you might call him. The other was smaller, a nice little horse.

That year Van sold about three hundred head of horses to Hi West, down at Big Canyon. His wife had all those police dogs she raised so he was buyin' dog food, but he kinda creamed 'em for his dude strings and the cavalry. Van put the three bays in the bunch to go to West's. I noticed 'em, see, and I asked him, "Why are you chickenin' horses like those geldings? They'd fit in anybody's cavvy."

"Aw," he said, "if they get away from you they'd go back to the Buffalo Hills."

"Well, then you'd know where they are and you can go get 'em anytime," I said. But the truth was they weren't Campstool horses. He branded with the Campstool and if they had had the Campstool on 'em he would have kept 'em in the cavvy. These horses were branded with an inverted quarter circle J on the shoulder, so he put 'em in the bunch to sell West.

We rode the regular saddle horses until we got to Round Hole on the Smoke Creek Desert and had the pratha off their range. The horses were getting easier to handle. There were lots of old saddle horses in the cavvy at Round Hole, good broke horses but too old to use anymore. Van was gonna to sell 'em to West. The cowboys rode 'em onto Big Canyon.

I had an old sorrel gelding in the bunch, so I jumped Van for a trade for the pretty bay horse. 'Course it didn't make any difference to him, so we traded and I left the bay with the cavvy that the boys would pick up on the way back.

We delivered the horses to Big Canyon. West expected the Bare Ranch cowboys to work 'em into separate bunches: cavalry horses, dude horses, culls for the dogs. For ten days we worked, cutting out anything West wanted to keep, mouthin' and brandin' 'em.

Greenbacks

He rides in darkness folding round. The ring of hoof ricochets off the desert floor. He looks behind to see. He's alone.

On the desert edge of uncharted dunes, trails bleed toward the springheart of the Buffalo Hills. Fox- or ferretlike and belly down, that's where he finds them feeding. The scent of horses fills him. The stallion sleeps standing. The lead mare stares him eye to eye then throws a warning in the dawning air. The run begins. He lets them have it and follows in a trot. Their dust by evening is barely lifting wisps. Footsore and thirsty, far off their home ground, they've given up escape.

He was a horseman. Horses taught him, fought him, made him whole. At times his only friends, they gave him legs and mind to catch their own.

He drove them through the tall pole gate of the compound. A woman on the porch pulled a hat on her brown hair, walked by rows and rows of wire kennels where German shepherds leaned against the wire, whining as she passed.

In the round corral the best were sorted. The others put off alone. Greenbacks folded in jeans pocket, thanks he didn't hear, he rode out past the dogs and imagined horses galloping hard (disappear in the screaming wire.) He drove his spurs into the fine hide of the bay but he could not ride fast enough. Behind, the shooting started.

When we got back from Big Canyon I broke the bay horse. I don't know how old he was. Up toward ten, I think. He showed no signs of ever bein' handled but he broke nice. He had a little white strip in his forehead about the size of a pencil, and two white socks behind and a little white circle on his ribs about the size of a dime. He was sure a keen booger. Jim Marr said he thought he was near a perfect horse as he'd ever seen.

You might think, Oh, this is a horse story. I've read this before. But it's not a horse story. It's a love story about a man who had ridden many horses, more horses than most can remember in all our dreams of horses.

It's a story of a man who used horses, their strength, their speed, their sense of how the world met, end to end, who knew their lives were shorter than most, longer than some.

It's a story of a man who cut the throat of a colt with his pocketknife because it floundered and fell behind. A man gone dry of love for all things, even horses, but not dry of wanting love.

Three geldings, cut as colts, turned out to grow, were gathered in the Buffalo Hills. One was the bloody color of the fox.

The unbroke horses swam a circle of the corral, the rapids, the dust. The blood bay slipped through them to the edge, stepped clear of the others, from its own dream into the dream of the man.

Man and horse in the corral, across tattered sand a silent dance began, foot spoke to hoof, shoulder to body, mind flowed into mind, thin as buffalo hide, one strand.

Never did the bay buck nor waste his time on fight. He gave up such things for the man's smell, touch, weight, pull of the bit on his tender mouth, spank of the stirrup against his shoulder, soft hat flapped over his eye, rope whisping by his ears, and the gate opening to the outside, to a trail across the Granites above the trees where colors changed and shadows drew to the shelter of stone.

At the top the world laid out wider than can be imagined if you have not stood where they stood to see the Black Rock Desert and the Smoke Creek Desert touch and go on alone.

The year went by this way. Easy days to begin, longer circles as summer moved on. The man had many horses in his string, some tougher, some as honest, but he looked forward to the blood bay.

At end of day he unsaddled, led the bay through the pasture gate. The bay didn't gallop to the other horses scattered on the meadow but walked to the sandy creek bank and folded his legs to roll the day's work from his back. Rose. Shook. Walked back to the man standing with his hand on the gate, the rope looped easy along his leg.

Van sent me to ride with Lyle Cook at Red Rock that summer. I put my horses I wasn't usin' in that rock-fenced pasture, but that rock fence didn't stop the bay. Of course he went right back to the Buffalos. We finished riding Cook's country and I joined the Gerlach outfit at Stockade.

Rodero at Stockade

Hi West had turned the horses he bought from Van on Tule Mountain. Some were old enough that they went back to their home range. Hi and Mrs. West rode up to meet the Marrs, the Bare Ranch outfit, and Dewey Parker at Stockade, to gather the Buffalo Hills again and work West's horses out.

At the Stockade in the Buffalos there's a high rimrock right above the corrals. There were two corrals, a big round corral on the south side and a little rock corral we used to catch the saddle horses in. The manatha of fifty or sixty head was in the big corral with sixty or seventy head of the Bare Ranch saddle horses. Dewey Parker was ridin' with us and he brought his saddle horses. The Marr boys were there and they brought saddle horses. So there was well over a hundred head of saddle horses alone.

That first morning we turned the cavvy out of the corral and they scattered around out on the flat below the rimrock to feed. Brin Marr had a big old bay horse he rode he called Arch, and he'd shake him every mornin', so Brin took him in this little rock corral to mount him. Somebody was a-horse-back in the gate. Brin got on Arch and he bucked around the corral. When he come to the gate, why, he just cut out right alongside the guy. He wasn't watchin' too close. Dewey Parker was sittin' on Canary, a pretty sorrel horse, just watchin'. There were some other guys there too. When Arch bucked by Dewey's horse, Canary threw his head down and bucked Dewey off. It was quite a sight. All those horses, and it was quite a crew too, Arch buckin' off through the country and Dewey with that white shirt on just flipped out there, hangin' on the Canary's reins.

The first night in camp at Stockade Happy Friel came down from Gerlach. He was the government trapper and he ran a line up through the Buffalo Hills. He had seen Van somewhere and Van told him if he needed a horse for coyote bait to shoot it, just as if he owned all of the horses in the Buffalo Hills. Friel said he had killed two horses that day and he thought one of 'em was a saddle horse because its tail was pulled.

The next morning we rode out the direction Friel had come the day before. Van got there before I did. He rolled the horse over to check the brand. I knew that horse the second I laid eyes on him. The bullet hit him right on that white spot on his ribs.

Old Van said, "Well, we'll get you one as good or better."

I didn't say anything.

Jim Marr said he was near a perfect horse
as he'd ever seen.

Hooves of Horses

Between Miller and Lux Spring and Horse Canyon twisted in the brush, the hooves of a horse still attached to the white, white of bones by tendons dried, strands of caramel candy pulled into tawny tapes against the marbled hoof, tipped up, a bowl or cup holding a rim of rain from the thunderstorm that graced us and now sweeps east to Virgin Valley.

Hooves in even pairs, commisures sidling the horny frog, heart-shaped, frayed as gardening fingers, dry as earth caked in the pretty curve of nail, bars support the sole, wall thick as a thumbnail is wide rounded by lava rock, sand, smooth as if polished with a jeweler's cloth. A good hoof to travel on.

Two-year-old, or three-, it's hard to say, but young and no more, dead, dismembered, head just in view over there, spine (here's the church, here's the steeple) ribs open (see all the people?).

How many hooves have I watched my father lift, trim to track straight and stay sound, shoe? I'd go along and turn the forge, air (my work drew) turned iron red hot enough to bend, shape. To those kids gathered round (my father could draw a crowd from his cuff, from behind my ear, from a wisp of cloud) I held court, explained no, it doesn't hurt the horse when the knife pares shavings, no, rasp grates ridges level, no, nails drive through the hoof wall to hold the shoe in place. No, I'd scoff with sudden upright posture, them twice my size and I so wise. I point out the frog knowing they would not believe me saying naw with eyes to my father who – wedging horseshoe nails in his grip of mouth like rays from sun – would shrug and nod. Ah, I was bright for a small girl with palomino hair. I'd lead the horse straight away, trot it back so he could pleasure in a just, swinging stride. How some old spoiled horse would drag on me then he'd step up and spook it to a trot. I'd go again, the horse improved in gait, set for work. We'd go home, Dad and me, a team, a pair. Him with money. Me with pride.

I caught up with John, him leading his horse, the ground leading him from that swale to that other drainage, from that hill white with diatoms to that far one bare of brush (a cove). In a place others regard as wasteland he sees the shoreline of an ancient lake alive with waterfowl, fringed by a savannah of palm, alder, fern, and metasequoia (a museum tree in the Americas now, but as a living tree, lost to humid Asia). He examines soil and bits of petrified wood, patrols drainage for bones and teeth of the beings that once flourished. And he finds them. We have boxes of them he works to identify and understand – joints of camels, giant ground sloth, jaws of rhino, deer, horses, and many still a mystery to him. He has the artist's vision, sees things others miss – same spot, same light, same opportunity. As a boy he struggled, caught between this flicker of interest and ranch work. Objects found were kept private, in pockets, boxes under the bed. Children rebuffed grow tenderly secretive and unstoppable. He didn't know why he felt at home, contented, inspired, until in my discovery of the desert he reached back to his own – open country.

He turns, a smile of *guess what I found,* says *open your hand,* eyes say *are you ready for this?* and in the basin of my palm he presses a thing – half a walnut shell, I would describe it so. *Can you guess?* he asks. *Merychippus.* Late Miocene. Dawn Horse. Three-toed. First grazer to harvest prairie grasslands. Long limbs with fused ulna/radius, tibia/fibula so it could gallop, turn without twisting wrist and ankle. Outdistanced predators like the bear-dog. Point from which all horse lineage evolved, extinct and living.

I knew hooves, held them in my palm to clean, doctor, simply hold the curve, so dense, so delicate, supporting the weight of transition, carrying the lifted stride of *Merychippus* – Dawn Horse. Hooves of horses. Flight of wings. And this one.

Part 4

... third, and last, when in the bridle he changes into the character he will have for life.

Arnold R. Rojas, *vaquero, historian, writer*

Whenever they had a dance in Eagleville the place would be just packed till you couldn't hardly wiggle, and the first thing you knew a brawl would bust out right square in the middle of the floor! Nine times out of ten Lige Langston would be right in the middle just a-sluggin' 'er out with one of the Dees boys. Well, if the band seen the fight start up, they'd stop playin' the song they were on and strike up "The Star Spangled Banner." Lige would hear it and straighten up, just like a man.

Lavelle

Whistler. Ah, he was a horse.

Whistler

*Old-timers say that Luis Lopez, the best
reinsman that ever rode on the Tejon, never
started to bit up a colt until the moon was
full. Horses bitted when it was tender were
invariably hard-mouthed runaways.*

Arnold Rojas

A year went by and I never heard a word out of Van
about a horse to replace the bay. When I went over to
Lost Creek earlier that spring there was a big sorrel horse
named Whistler in the cavvy Van gave me to ride. He was in
Jimmy Short's string and Jimmy was a little leery of the
horse. He had got the horse to runnin' away. Outside of that I
didn't know much about him. I rode him twice. I rode him
one day at Granite Creek. He was a high-powered horse.
Spike Malone broke him and he never rode a horse with
chaps or spurs either one. 'Course that's the way I rode all
the time so that's the way I was ridin' him. You didn't need
spurs, I found out right away. And chaps, of course, that was
somethin' else. The wind might blow up one of your wings
and you couldn't tell what he might do.

I had a few head of steers I sold to Waltz but I had to

deliver 'em to Deep Hole. I saw Van over there and he said he left Whistler in the field over at Squaw Valley. "If you want him you can go over there and get him," he told me. 'Course I'd seen Spike ridin' him and I rode him twice and I figured after I got used to him I could get along with him all right. I was pretty tickled. That night I rode over to Dewey Parker's and I told him Van said I could have old Whistler.

"God! I wouldn't take *him*."

"Why?"

"They had a rodeo over at Gerlach on the Fourth of July and Van took some horses in there and bucked 'em out. Whistler was in the bunch. I tell ya, that bugger can buck! An Indian from Nixon saw him and tried to trade Van a good broke horse for Whistler. I guess Van agreed to the trade."

"If I can get to Squaw Valley before that Injun does, Whistler's gonna be my horse."

Next morning I saddled up and got the heck out of there. I rode to Squaw Valley. The horses were in the field, so I corralled 'em, caught Whistler, saddled him, and rode him in the corral. Heck, he went right off. But I had to go out in the field and down about three hundred yards and through a gate to be outside. After I got on him he run and bucked a little bit but it didn't amount to anything. He was mine from then on. I'll tell you, you were *a-horseback*. The days wasn't too long for that walloper. You could work cows,

rope calves right outside on him. Long as you paid attention and did your job, he'd do his. He was A number one.
Ah, he was a *horse*.

I'd had one wreck with Whistler, back before I traded for
him. We were branding calves up on the north end of the
Granites. Wagontire, they called it. After we finished we
were moving to Clear Creek, above Deep Hole. Van sent us
off south to ride on the way down to Clear Creek. There
were big boulders, big, the size of a house scattered through
the junipers. Quite a few of 'em. I was ridin' him with spurs
and he was never ridden with spurs. Well, goin' down
through there he got to runnin' and buckin', goin' pretty
good, and that old mountain is a steep sucker. As straight
down as it can be.

Well, down through those darned trees you couldn't see
ahead of you much. When we broke out of the trees we were
right on the edge of a rimrock. Down below was like you
took a monstrous bulldozer and scooped out a huge hole and
filled it with boulders – and I mean *boulders!* – and just
filled the bottom up. And way out there was a little clearing,
'bout the size of an ordinary room. Whistler never hesitated
a second. He jumped straight out into the air just as high
and as far as he could. By gosh, he missed those rocks!

When he landed, he fell on his right side and drove my

right shoulder into the ground, but as soon as he hit the ground, why, he got right up and I did too. I looked back up at Red. He was up there where Whistler had taken off. He asked if I was hurt and I said no, not very bad anyway. Whistler just went a little way from where he fell and was standin' there. 'Course, he was probably shook up, too.

I had a brand new riata on my saddle that Van had given me the day before and it was sixty or seventy feet long. It wouldn't even have come close to reachin' Red. He said, "If I had a rifle, I'd shoot that sucker right where he stands."

He come down around there and we walked down off this place and went out on a ridge. We decided we'd trade horses. I wasn't sure I could get back on Whistler with my arm bunged up. Red was ridin' a little snaffle bit horse that seemed pretty gentle. I started to unsaddle Whistler and put my saddle on Red's horse, but Red rode Whistler before and didn't get along with him, so I just reined him up and turned him loose. I told Red to ride down to Clear Creek and get that old Ford and come up and get me in the car. By the time he got back up there, man! I was stove up. I was laid up about twenty-nine days after that wreck. I went into Reno and stayed with Ma.

Whistler. Aw, he'd buck with you every time you got on him, if you got on and off him fifty times a day, but he was a good horse. I just knew that.

Mary Pruitt Steel

I wish I'd asked her how she came to love the man named Pruitt. Wasn't she expecting more than he had tied up in his bedroll? Does a woman know, after all, the slip of first-run fabrics, smooth-grained leather shoes with piping round the ankle, lace-trimmed underclothes, and never desire them? Can she dream a scent, a jeweled hair comb, a flower grown and named for her alone, leather gloves soft as the skin behind her ear and trade them straight across for a man to ride beside and raising livestock in a country that can live without her?

I had no way of knowing she was Mary when I saw a woman standing at the top of Echo Canyon. She was no visitor, no stranger like I was that first year, I could tell that right away in her easy way of standing, in her eyes as much at home as the colors and the shadows. The desert seemed to know her. Did I hear the canyon call out as I rode up the draw, bounce her name from one black slick face to strike another sharp as sunlight? Or was it a hawk that screeched in great surprise?

Three hundred sixty-five times the years past since she left the desert, times hours dark and light, times seasons frozen shut in silence, bathed in wild bees seeking flowers, times breath, times heartbeat, times chance, times, times. How many stars? How many grains of sand? And in the ocean, how many fishes' tears? I don't believe in coincidence but I do trust destiny – it slowed me up or sped me forward to this meeting.

She stood beside the car, a breeze as hot as summer lifting

her dark hair. I drank water from her dipper. We talked of nothing and later on, when I understood who she was, wished I had asked her about love and truth and honor.

My first day on the desert after running with the horses, John and I rode east past Ten Mile Spring, past the cave wall where a Basque herder carved 1905 under his name – A. Urell – past the horse corrals to where the canyon narrows. Where the rock walls slanted to the ground in a gallery of lichen – green, orange, gold – the sage broke open in a clearing. A small bench stood beside a stream. Aspen leaves were flakes of sunshine broken loose and scattered on its dark reflection. John said further on were beaver dams and further on were fish.

The one-room cabin was built of cottonwood logs, twisted, tapered, peeling bark like snakeskin hanging on a rock in August, chinked wide and narrow, tight as a beaver lodge. Smaller, straighter poles supported the sod roof and made the cellar under a low mound out back. Across the stream, in bedrock shaded by the aspen, a rounded hole gaped open. Someone had chipped an oven into the stone. Mary could light a fire to warm the rock, slide a dutch oven filled with roast or stew down into the hole, scatter a few coals on the lid, and supper would be ready when she and Pruitt finished work and rode home.

Hunters found it: half-burned paper plates, sardine cans wrenched open in a V, and whiskey bottles spilled out. John stepped off his horse and handed me his reins. He scooped out the oven by double handfuls, found a piece of tin in the brush, and used it as a shovel to bury the trash.

We tied the horses, sat on the bench, and ate our lunch. He

told the story of Mary's life in the cabin. She and Pruitt came here, bride and groom, to build a ranch. In the second year of their marriage she found stolen calves penned up in a box canyon. Tracks where the wire was stretched led her off the Rock Springs Table. She followed them down the rocky switchback, already telling Pruitt in her mind that a thief rode in their country. Hope turned back at the south gate of their horse pasture. The thief she followed just turned his horse loose and was waiting for her by the corral. She fixed supper, washed the dishes, lay with Pruitt till he slept. The moon rose late but Mary knew the trail. She pulled the wires down, drove the calves out of the canyon, and rode away.

I stepped into a room small as a playhouse. I could touch the ceiling, by simply turning reach the stove, table, screened cupboard, bed. Its frame of rough-cut poles was bound by rawhide knotted square, rusted springs coiled bare and rigid. The window above the bed was opened out. A mirror framed in green chipped paint was broken in by one blow: a hammer or a fist. On the shelf beside the stove – a fruit jar with its store of colored buttons, a can of baking powder, a Searchlight cookbook pack-rats spoiled with stains of scent. There were two settings of chalk blue dishes, a mixing bowl. Nothing anyone would care to carry home.

I've spent since then thinking about a woman who knew right from wrong and had the strength to live it – and how she came to wait for me at Echo Canyon.

Gathering cattle on the desert let me learn it, outside in. I had a job to do but it was exploration. I often envied the herder walking slowly with his sheep feeling the earth against toe-arch-heel, fingertips in morning dew. From the ground he sees every angle of the earth. An antelope kid swift behind the doe. Mariposa lilies, white with tongues of violet. Lynx watching from the brush. Creamy agate shading to lead, or chocolate brown that deepens nearly rose. A herder found a projectile point chipped from fire opal. It lies on black velvet in a museum now – icy iridescence glowing in minute petals of conchoidal fractures – to celebrate the art of killing. I missed a great deal on horseback in a long trot, looking for the moving red or black of cows. I also made a gain.

Mary came back to the desert. First she returned to Badger Camp to cook for Alkali, spring and fall. John remembered her being there the first year he was allowed to go along. The days moving cattle were too long for a boy of five. He was left in camp with Mary. After she cleaned up breakfast, loaded the lunch and branding box in the Dodge truck, the two of them drove over Badger Mountain to meet the crew at Rock Springs, Cherry, Cottonwood, Wheeler, or Domingo.

She sang to him as they bumped along. He can't recall the songs, just her across the cab looking over at him now and then, singing. She was nice, that's what he remembered.

> *Gonna dance with my dolly*
> *with a hole in her stocking*
> *while her knees keep a-knocking*
> *and her toes keep a-rocking.*
> *Gonna dance with my dolly*
> *with a hole in her stocking.*
> *Gonna dance by the light of the moon.*

Mary returned a second way – my mind's companion as I learned the country. Devaney's still in the rocks above the spring, stashed bottles greened and amethyst by years since Prohibition. Rock corrals, house, and even the outhouse made of teetering rock at Gooch Camp. The horse trap called the Penitentiary. Wisteria wound above an abandoned cabin door blew a sweetened breeze into the quiet. I wanted to know more about Mrs. Perry. I'd heard she begged her husband for a place to stay put – a home – so he took up a homestead fifty miles from Surprise at Wall Canyon and left her with the children while he went freighting up the Ruby Mine Road to Idaho. They said he'd come back every year with supplies and leave her pregnant again but happy to have a solid little frame house by the wash where she could raise her children. On one annual visit her husband rose from the table saying, "Anyone who wants to get rich, come with me." No child stirred. He left for Mexico. They never saw him again. A Swedish rock mason happened by. He built a two-story house across the swale and, when he left the country, gave the house to her. I like to think he loved her but I might be wrong. Mary would know.

Mary agreed to wed again, a military man. He moved her from the desert for good. But she was there for me. She was the only woman I knew who rode that Badger country alongside the men, competent as they were, as much a part of it as anyone. I followed her spirit every morning. One day Mary stepped her horse aside and gave the trail to me.

Part of me wanted to move out to her cabin – still does – to give it chance to be a home again, fill the wood with the smell of dinner cooking, let the smoke rise through the grove of aspens, sit on her little bench and see how the solid canyon walls juxtapose the stars. Just be there, silent as the canyon, steady as the spring that moves past her side door. Maybe right the wrong. Spin out her dream. But I didn't go back. It never came right.

Lige, Spud Murphey, and the Long Arm of the Law

A truck comin' out of Home Camp nearly run over us! We had to hit the brush! There was two guys in the thing, but we didn't know 'em. The back of their truck was piled with stuff, but we didn't think too much of it at the time. Spud cussed 'em good, pulled back on the road, and we went on. Well, when we got to Home Camp the place had been robbed. Food, bedding, everything. They took everything that wasn't nailed to the floor. Spud and me jumped right into the truck and took after those guys. We could see their dust out on the main road. They was rippin' up the country. Spud poured on the coal and we finally caught up with 'em. 'Course we couldn't see for the dust, but Spud pulled around 'em and forced 'em into the barrow pit. Well, we had a little conversation, you might say, right there. We told 'em they better just follow along behind us, 'cause we were takin' 'em in to the law and turn 'em in. So they said they would. I was drivin' that time and Spud was watchin' out the back window and pretty soon he says they started fallin' behind. So I stops and they catch up with us. Well, they had altogether a different attitude. They said we didn't have anything on 'em. No evidence, they say. So I got to lookin' and one of 'em had climbed into the back of the rig and threw all the stuff out. Then they got real smart with us. We was bound and determined to take 'em in, and they was a-draggin' their feet. So this little guy kinda paired off with Spud and this other one started in on me. We got right into it and every time this guy got up, I'd just knock him down. Finally, he'd had enough, but Spud was havin' trouble keepin' even with his, so I kinda had to help him out a bit. We finally got all the stuff gathered up and got 'em into the law, but that time we split 'em up so they couldn't brew up any more tricks.

About People You Know

By Irvine Grove

Surprise Valley Journal
Thursday, October 29, 1953

Our Wild West Days aren't over in this part of the country. Not by a jug full. The other evening a pick-up with two men in it stopped at one of our business establishments and, after mentioning the name of a well-known Reno doctor as having told them to inquire about the shortest way into Home Camp, and being directed by our courteous businessman, proceeded to said camp. Upon finding no one at home the men helped themselves to everything they could find, including a barrel of gas, a heavy waterproofed tarp, a rifle, radio and almost all of Spud Murphey's clothes and started jubilantly on their way only to meet Lige Langston and Spud coming back home. The two custodians of Home Camp property immediately wanted to know "how come?" No reasonable answer being forthcoming, Lige proceeded to "whop" one of the men, but good, while Spud kept his eyes on the other one. Incidentally, they were both carrying guns. Some of the stolen stuff was unloaded and the men tried to make their get away. Lige and Spud brought them into the valley and turned them over to law officers. It is thought they were traveling in a stolen car. When someone asked Lige if he wasn't afraid of them shooting him he replied: "Nope! I was just too darn mad to think of anything but giving them so and so's a good licking."

Afterbirth

Meadow Morn foaled in May. We saw a dark shadow brush beside her at daybreak. John rode out to check and soon I could see the mare band loping toward the corrals, so I fixed the gates. Foals are born early in the spring or should be if they're meant to compete in age events at shows or on the track. A month or two sets a bloom that's hard to overlook. If the horse is to be used for work or pleasure riding, never mind. The weather in this country can be a serious consideration. Though February can feel like April, April can also blow a blizzard that chills deep as December. We breed our mares to foal on clover and we've had good luck.

Meadow Morn hadn't cleaned yet. The afterbirth dragged behind like a gutted animal caught by a leg. A cow can drag a nasty hunk around for a week till it's good and ripe, maybe snag it on a brush and pull it loose, maybe just wear it in two, and never take a hot breath. But a horse is different, delicate and warm blooded. Twelve hours can be serious for a mare.

I started for the house to telephone the vet. He's seventy-five miles away and would have to plan his day around this call. A truck came up the road, slowed when the dogs rushed out. John introduced me to the man in the truck as Peachy Van Norman. Charlie and Philip Van Norman were horsemen well known to me. This was a brother I didn't know.

People do that sort of thing in ranch country, they just drive in. I like it. When they catch me off guard I don't fuss over having just dumped an armload of laundry on the kitchen table. I shove papers and clutter aside as if they're part of the family. And as for food, it's potluck.

Meadow Morn was in a big stall in the barn. We leaned our arms on the pole gate and looked at the foal, a tiny dream of the mare. Peachy asked, "Got any turpentine?"

"I think so. Somewhere."

"Go get it and a jar lid."

"Turpentine," I thought as I rummaged through the old ice-box in the shop. Clean paint off my hands. In the old days: paint a sore throat, slosh it on an arthritic knee, soak a rag and wrap a neck for whooping cough. Home remedies might be okay for desert horses but this was a registered mare. I wasn't doctoring her with something from the hardware store. As soon as Peachy Van Norman left, I was calling the vet. I was busy wondering what other jobs I could lump into this long distance call to spread out the cost when a voice at my shoulder brought me around.

"Find the turpentine?"

Actually, I had the green can in my hand.

"Good. Get a lid."

I'd never seen this man before and I was going to the house for a jar lid like a scolded child. The vet's wife said he'd be on his way as soon as he finished spaying the dog he was working on. I tossed the mayonnaise lid in the air as I walked back to the barn.

Meadow Morn was nearing her twelve-hour mark and showing distress. Her neck, chest, and flanks were slick with sweat. The raw sheet draped her hind legs. John looked at me, shrugged, and got a halter. Peachy measured two tablespoons of turpentine into the lid and held it up to her stomach, an inch or so below her navel. He withdrew the lid. It was empty. He took the halter off and stood back. Nothing happened for about five minutes and then the mare slung her head back along her side. She was nervous and uncomfortable. She stomped and kicked, then she whirled and kicked again. The afterbirth slipped and, with the next kick, went flying. John and I stared in disbelief as Meadow Morn turned to smell the ragged membrane.

John had a flash of insight. A couple winters before a big pine went down in the cow lot. After months of long hay the cows were hungry for anything green and some of them ate the pine needles. Aborted calves lay out on the snow like rose petals. Turpentine.

Peachy said he had to go. We walked him to his truck.

"I hear you went to visit Dad," Peachy said as he shook my hand.

"Huh? Oh, yes. Yes I did." I was wondering if I could catch the doc before he left the office.

"How was he?"

"Amazing, really. It's as if Little High Rock happened yesterday."

"I wish he could forget it. It was only a few days out of his life."

I was suddenly aware of the bad memories I'd left stirring in a fine old man and I was sorry.

"It's all right. You weren't the first and you won't be the last. I just wish people could remember him for what he was, a damned good cowman."

We never saw Peachy Van Norman again.

Lost Creek Horse Thief's Paradise

Ira Millsap ran horses out toward the Coppersmiths, west of the Flat. They was all mixed up together with everybody's horses. He branded with a quarter circle open AL. Before Ira joined up for World War One he deeded his horses over to his mother. She was livin' out at his place, I guess. A guy named George Brooks probably intended to buy 'em, but somehow he got the bill of sale from Mrs. Millsap and never paid any money.

I was up at the Marrs' when Ira came up there to see me. Maybe Brooks meant to pay up for the Millsap horses but it had been almost ten years and he never paid anything. All this time Brooks was still brandin' the horses. Ira said he had been to all the judges and district attorney, anybody who might have some authority or know somethin' about what you'd have to do in a case like this but he couldn't find out anything from anybody.

Brooks had originally recorded Ira's iron in California but he had let it run out in the meantime and he had moved the horses to Fox Mountain in Nevada, up around Home Camp. There were quite a few on the Coppersmiths, Cottonwood, and just everywhere.

Since Ira couldn't get any legal authorization to gather the horses he decided to just go ahead and do it, then get the authorization. He wanted to hire me to gather 'em. I said, "Well, if that's the way the thing is, why, I'll gather 'em." So he brought out some of his nephews and guys from Reno. I had saddle horses enough for all of us and there was a Brooks horse or two that was broke. One black horse that run in the Coppersmiths, especially. I knew all the horses, most of 'em anyway.

Before Ira come out there he went to Susanville and got the iron recorded on the California side in his name and, of course, he didn't do anything about Nevada because they weren't recorded over there before anyway.

He said he thought we could start gatherin' in the Coppersmiths. I said I didn't think I'd start over there. The Coppersmiths are in California and he had the iron recorded in his name over on that side of the line. I said, "They're your horses now, or you can claim 'em. But we'll go to Fox Mountain before anybody finds out about it and I know we could get a dandy bunch in one day over there, before Brooks finds out what we're doin'." So we went east to Fox Mountain, Nevada.

We had quite a time. Those amateurs he brought out from town knew how to handle a horse a little, but they never done anything like that before. We done all right. We got enough for a carload in one day. Brought 'em across the Flat, over Tuledad, and shipped 'em out of Ravendale. Ira took care of 'em from there.

After we got the first carload shipped I knew we'd have to figure out something different. We didn't have very good luck the first day and we probably wouldn't've gotten any if the horses hadn't been pretty gentle.

Ira said, "How would it be if I just pay so much a day for every horse you gather and *you* get somebody to help you?" That sounded like a good idea so I got old Spike Malone to help me and we started in. We split the money. If we got two horses in a day, he'd get five dollars and I'd get five dollars. That's the way we worked it.

It was too darned far to ride that Grass Valley country from home at Duck Flat, so I went to see Ed Waltz. He owned the Gerlach Ranch and run over all that country. I hoped he'd let us stay at one of his camps, maybe. He not only let us stay, he furnished the grub and sent the Gopher out to cook for us. He wanted those horses off his country as bad as we did.

We started from Lost Creek and rode Fox Mountain, all that country in there. After we got that done we rode into Clover Creek and made a circle, just kept comin' on around.

Then we moved to Home Camp. Old Domingo had Home Camp then. There was some Millsap horses in that country and I knew most of 'em.

When we'd get some horses gathered we'd take 'em out to the Flat. We couldn't leave 'em in our field or somebody'd see 'em. Old John Erramouspe owned a big field on Cottonwood Mountain, so we fixed the fence and paid him by the day. We rode Home Camp and then the Murphy Place for a day or two. We could reach Brigger Mountain easy from there, and the Coppersmiths we could reach from home, so we finished up the country. We missed one horse over in that Fox Mountain country. He was runnin' off down toward Red Mountain. I heard of him afterwards. We left the brown mare that was runnin' at Garden Lake. She was the only one over there that I knew of, a big old gentle mare. We just didn't take time to go get her. He had two mares that run on top of Cottonwood Mountain that'd weigh sixteen hundred if they'd weigh a pound. Black mares. Good ones. We got all of 'em.

Brooks had heard about us a-gatherin' the horses so he was out there after us, but he was about ten days behind. We could check up on him. Somebody's tell us every place he'd go. We just kept ahead of him.

We had another carload ready to ship so I had to go into Eagleville to telephone Ira. While I was there I went over to Louis Grove's garage to get gas. Brooks was there at the garage. 'Course I didn't know it. He come out and jumped me about runnin' his horses. I don't remember what I told him but I gave him some kind of spiel and he said he was comin' out to my place in the morning to see what I had out there.

Spike and me, we decided that we'd be gathered up and gone when he got out there. We drove the last carload over to Madeline the next mornin'. From then on we called our place Lost Creek Horse Thief's Paradise.

I can remember Lige ridin' into Eagleville on some big old snorty desert horse when I was a kid. He was just like a movie star to me.

Peter Ytcaina, *merchant*

The Album

The women in Lige's life are held in place by black paper tabs glued down. In a garden Pearl and her daughters stand within a grove of her boys, Lige, the oldest, the tallest, the buckaroo. There are several pictures of Pearl. She was all things to Lige – faith, endurance, strength, laughter. He loved her without hesitation but never found her devotion in a woman of his own.

The divorce seekers have their own pages. Bessie, Jerkwater Jones, all of them he saddled horses for and danced with in the simple cabin and sent back home with a different idea of men. Jo Washington, who could "drink more whiskey than a mule could pack," died at the ranch. He didn't know why, but when he said it, there was a pause that reminded him there were many things he would never understand. Packages came on the stage with photographs folded in letters, a published story about a branding on the ranch in which one woman visitor wrote about the cowboys "taking the manly stature of the bull calves." One woman sent a Victrola and dance records. They remembered him for a while.

Paul Fite and Lige and others who were not named are riding bad broncos and winning prizes. Dad Hicks poses with his violin in a flour sack, a rifle in the other hand to keep people away. He looks as tall as Lige remembered him.

There are three pictures of his first wife, Francine. Their marriage was brief. The camera couldn't get close enough to read her mystery, which first fascinated Lige and then drove him away. She denies film an image of her secret agonies.

I find only two pictures of Lige's second wife, Etta Harris, a widow eight years older than Lige, with two young boys and a ranch that needed tending. It is said she was a woman who, if you owed her a dollar, she wanted that dollar. And if she owed you one, she wanted to pay it. One picture was taken after their wedding in 1942 outside Pearl's house in Reno. She is laughing hard, as though something surprisingly good has come her way.

She took her brother's advice, "Don't let Lige get away!" Their marriage endured for forty-two years.

Don't let Lige get away.

There's a story I can remember my folks tellin' about
Etta and Lige. It happened when I was just a kid. The
Community Church in Eagleville was in need of some
major repairs, a new roof, I think, and the collection
plate wasn't bringin' in enough. So the ladies held a
fund-raiser one Sunday after services. They invited all
the ranchers, everybody. Lige and Etta went, of course,
and took the boys. After supper and the program they
asked for pledges of one hundred dollars. Lige was one of
the first to raise his hand. Well, Etta threw a fit right
there in front of everybody. He wasn't givin' away her
hard-earned money to no church! I don't think Etta'd
ever seen Lige choke down a bunch-quittin' cow and
grind dirt into her eyes, but I had. Lige faced Etta down
in his quiet way that made the hair stand up on your
neck. Then one of her boys jumps up and shouts, "You
can't speak to my mother like that!" Lige said, "Sit down
or I'll knock you down." Lige wrote a check on the spot.
That was the end of that.

John

Francine was comin' up the sidewalk one day and Lige come along. He pulls that blue truck of his right over to the curb. The window was down an' he leans across an' says somethin' to Francine. I couldn't hear what it was, a' course, I was clear up to the post office but she stands there lookin' in at him, stiff as a hoe handle. He was doin' all the talkin', I could see that. She's real thin, you know. Been doctorin' here lately. Haven't heard what for. But for all me, that drinkin' does take hold of a person after a while. Well, he reaches across the seat and the door swings open but she still just stands there for the longest time. Pretty soon she gets in the truck and Lige starts off up the street. Well, they didn't go fifty feet when here comes Etta right up behind 'em. She musta followed him up from the ranch. You won't believe this, but she lays on the horn like she's callin' in for a fire and never lets off, no way! Everybody's gawkin' at 'em goin' up the street that way. I jumps into my rig and follows 'em too, so I seen the whole thing. Lige pulls right up to the hospital just as unconcerned as if he's out for a Sunday drive. He hops out and hurries around to Francine's side, opens the door, takes her hand, and helps her into the hospital. Etta's out there just a-poundin' on that horn. Well, some of the nurses come out to see what's goin' on but when they see it's Etta they just flap their hands at her to shut it up and they go back inside. But Etta don't slack off one bit. Lige takes his own sweet time in there an' when he comes out he never even looks at Etta, just gets into his truck and drives off toward home. Etta's right after him, still layin' on the horn with both feet. Last I seen of 'em they was headed south. I wouldn'-ta wanted to be in her shoes when he got her home, not for all the world. If they ain't a pair! That marriage was where the rattlesnake met the mule.

the town gossip

Etta was not a happy person. She was so critical of Lige. Last time we were up there she says, Look at what he's wearin'. He's got a brown necktie on with a blue shirt. And I said, That's what wives are for. And she said, He makes me tired! He's so stubborn! And I says, It runs in our family.

Jessie

I was a pretty good guy until I signed the ranches over to the boys, then I was an s.b.

Marriage, Cows, and Heroes

In the 1950s Lige left the ranch he had managed and tripled in size for Etta, and her two sons took over when they were old enough. It was no secret there were hard feelings between the boys and their stepfather.

Lige and Etta moved to a house they built in Cedarville, and he called on John's father, Walter Hussa, to ask for a job range-riding for Alkali Cattle Company. The three partners, Walter, Lee Heryford, and P. B. Harris, drove Lige out to Badger to get an idea of the country.

John pushed into the back seat of the Buick between Lige and Lee. Going over Forty-nine Pass he pulled a leather lacing from his pocket and tried to lay a button around a stick the way he had seen Lige do on a pair of rawhide reins. "Now, John, don't bother Lige," Walter would say when the boy interrupted the men's conversation, and Lige laughed, "Aw, he's no bother." Then his big hands would slide over John's little ones to direct the string in its course. "A feller's got to ask questions if he's gonna learn."

Lige went to work for the company. He was far away from his old buckaroo friends but horsemen anywhere are friends.

When John turned twelve Lige took him to Badger for part of that summer and every summer until he left for college.

A man in camp cooks different than a woman in her kitchen. More grease poppin' and a dust of flour your boots track around, a dipper hangin' above the water pail. The smell of the country comin' in through the open door, coffee, bacon carryin' down the meadow.

Lige always cleaned up the kitchen before we left camp, so while we'd eat, the dishwater was heating, the pan sputtering, doin' a little dance on the stove. No extra dishes, no table scarves to mess up. Jam in a jar and pancakes swimmin' in the juice of stewed prunes and raisins right on your plate.

We never knew who'd be in camp when we got in at night. Folks were always comin' out to visit Lige. They'd never think of goin' to the house in town. Might be rock hounds or hunters or other buckaroos, they'd just stop by. We'd have a big time.

John

John and Polly, the Runaway Mare

When I was a kid I liked to stay a-horseback. I guess
that hasn't changed. When I was about twelve Lige and
I were riding, helping Laxague gather the east side of
the valley, from the Long Ranch back toward Forty-nine
Holding Field. I was above the tavern at Stateline, overlapping with Lige coming from the south, when I saw
him up on the sidehill in pursuit of a critter. He disappeared over the brow of a pretty steep little hill along the
drainage of Forty-nine Creek. By the time I got over
there he had his rope on a wild steer. Sometimes cattle
get scared and they just take off running. I stayed back
behind the steer to keep him moving so Lige wouldn't
have to drag him. We were trying to get him to the top of
the break so he could see the big bunch of cattle ahead
and go toward them. I had my rope down, of course, a
kid's always ready to rope something, when the steer
kinda lodged behind a brush. I started beatin' on his
rear end with my rope, trying to get him to break loose
and get moving. He was a big steer, had to weigh eight
hundred to a thousand pounds, and Lige's horse was
gettin' a little leg-weary holdin' him. Being a young

fella, I wasn't paying too much attention about whether or not my horse was in position, and when Lige let his turns slide the steer kinda folded around the little palomino mare I was riding. Polly was real sensitive to a rope and when it hit her in the chest she blew up and bucked right into that steer. My spur rowel hung up on Lige's riata. Her and me ended up cuttin' his rope right in two, about six inches from the hondo. The swinging button broke out of the shank and my spur went sailin' out through the air. Polly bucked me off, of course. I couldn't ride one side of her when she got her mind set on buckin', and she knocked the steer off his feet. We both ended up on the ground when the dust settled. I was layin' alongside of that steer in the brush, both of us on our backs, the air out of him and the air out of me. My mare was headed off Forty-nine Mountain, still buckin' and kickin' at the rope hung on the saddle horn.

Lige was sittin' up there on his horse just a-laughing his head off. He coiled up what was left of his riata and he asks, "Well, what do you want me to do?" "I guess go after my horse," I says. By this time the steer had rolled up on his belly and was beginning to get his bearings and Lige grinned, "What about that steer there?" "I'll take care of him" I says. So he trotted off to get Polly.

I was on my hands and knees looking at the steer

through this big brush and he was on the other side eye-balling' me. There was no doubt he was on the fight, so I figured the best thing for me to do was just hold quiet. Pretty soon he got to his feet. He made one sashay at me as he came around the brush and then he took off. By the time Lige got back the steer was long gone. We never saw him again.

Lige loved to tell that story. I'd see him in town and he'd get tickled thinking about me and that steer, both of us down on the ground on our bellies, lookin' through that big brush at each other. People always had time to visit in those days so somebody would be there on the side-walk with him and he'd tell about Polly and the wreck on the old Forty-nine.

The first time I saw that little mare was in the '50s when the Golden Hotel burned. The men had been fightin' the fire all day and they were just mopping up, hoses strung all over the street. They were washing 'em off, rolling 'em up. All the sudden we hear a big commotion comin' from the north end of town. Here comes this horse run-nin' full out draggin' something, totally out of control. When she got up to us the men got her headed off and stopped her. She had about thirty foot of rope tied around her neck, draggin' a tire. Polly never got over that fear of a rope. She belonged to the Sweet family, but she got to outsmarting the kids so I got her in my string of horses. Lige helped me with her but I don't think she ever relaxed when there was a rope around. 'Course that business with the steer on Forty-nine Mountain didn't do her any good. Oh, I roped on her, branded and so on, but I always had to be on my guard riding Polly. I used to sing that old song, "That Palomino Pal of Mine," but I don't think it made much of an impression on Polly.

Lige loved to tell the story about mc and Polly.

Lige was always a gentleman, even when there was just men around. Never said anything off-color, but one time he gave me something to think about. I came highballin' around the saddle shed in a big rush and Lige was standin' out there a ways with his back to me. Like kids do I blurted out, "Whatcha doin' Lige?" He looked over his shoulder as he buttoned up his pants. "Shakin' hands with the unemployed," he says.

John

The majority of Lige's work built on caring for the cattle, moving them to fresh feed, cleaning springs, putting out salt, doctoring, scattering bulls. No glamour. Just riding, bringing young horses, and a boy, along in that slow pace that passes learning through the invisible borders of work.

In the 1950s the last big gathering of horses took place in that country. Harry Wilson had had a horse permit since he took over the Smoke Creek Desert Division from the estate of Miller and Lux. The Umbrella brand horses owned a reputation for being tough. The high desert weeded them out as sure as it did any wild species. But once the horse gave way to horsepower Wilson's management focused on beef and his horse numbers got out of control. The refuge boss gave Wilson's the word to clean their horses off the Gooch tableland and the south country toward Summit Lake Mountain.

John was the kid holding the manatha while Lige, Billy McCluskey, and the Wilsons ran the horses. One day as they were riding over from camp he told John about running horses with Billy.

I was out at Alkali one fall and rode with 'em runnin' horses. We got clear into Long Valley from out east. They was camped at Bull Creek and we rode from there. We was up there in the Black Hills, that country between Home

Camp and Antelope Flat. I was with Billy McCluskey. We jumped a bunch of ten or twelve, and when we come up on 'em, they was headed east, right across Antelope Flat, three or four miles over to Nellie Spring Mountain. And Nellie Spring Mountain runs north for miles. All we did was start 'em. That was the way they wanted to run. Billy just sat there and watched 'em. He didn't follow 'em or anything. After they got over there to Nellie Spring Mountain they took north and followed right along the foot of the mountain quite a ways, then they turned and came across to the Black Hills. Billy took off, and when they got to the Black Hills, he was waitin' for 'em. They run all this distance with us just watchin' 'em. He had an idea where to go and he was there. He just fell in behind 'em and that's the way he won that bunch.

Time after time I watched him ride out on a ridge and maybe start a bunch and they might head out across country and he'd just sit there and watch 'em quite a little while. Pretty soon, he might go any direction, just some other direction, and you wouldn't see him or the horses, either one, until maybe an hour or two later, and he'd be with 'em.

Billy was a half-breed Indian but he seemed about half horse. He went to work for Miller and Lux when he was sixteen years old at Soldier Meadows breakin' broncos. I'd guess that was around the time I was born, 1908 or so. He said he just stayed right there at the corrals and that's all he did was break horses. They'd bring him a bunch and he'd get 'em started so you could ride 'em and they'd bring him a new bunch. Range horses. Wild horses. Halter break 'em, saddle 'em, get on and off 'em, so you could do your work. 'Course they had cowboys to ride 'em. I don't think it would be exaggeratin' a bit to say he started a thousand horses.

The last time that I rode with him he had that bleedin' ulcer. Heck! He couldn't eat enough breakfast to keep a jay-bird alive and then throw up off his horse and just ride all day. I don't know how he did it, but he just did.

One of the buckaroos highgraded a jug of wine and brought it into camp. He filled everybody's cup and handed one to Billy. Billy took a big swig and shook his head. "Coffee's the staff of life . . . but this is better."

Pete Crystal, *buckaroo*

Wilson's horsebackers got help from Ted Barber and his souped-up Super Cub. Even wild horses couldn't outsmart his airplane. Dangling from a thirty-foot rope tied around the belly of the plane through the open cockpit, a five-gallon can dragged in the brush to turn a bunch toward the trap. Above that can were a dozen others, smashed by the job, adding to the noise. Ted was not foolish, but to a young boy he seemed fearless, standing the cub on the tip of its wing, pivoting, and falling back into position, as if he flew over open fields that stretched for placid miles, not down the sucking high canyons and gorges of that rough Nevada desert.

Hundreds of horses were gathered into Alkali Canyon. Stallions fought night and day trying to keep their bands separate. John could not take his eyes from them, from the men riding with him. They were the same in a way, the men and the horses, trying to hold onto the freedom that was their life.

On the last night John walked down the meadow fence, his hand feeling the smooth and the knot of the poles, willow limbs wired upright, stockade-style. Some horses were lying down, footsore, leg weary. Some were grazing or drinking or standing asleep like gentle saddle horses. The fence turned their freedom inward. He stood at the gate. Something in him wanted to throw it back. His hand found the chain, each link as big as his fist. But he was proud to be one with the men who built the fence, who forged the chain, who gathered the range horse in.

He dropped the hook and walked back to the house. In the dancing shadows of the kerosene lamps he lay out on his bedroll listening to the men until he fell asleep.

A lot of guys watched me work with horses as I was growing up, learning. But they couldn't see what I was trying to accomplish, or if they could, they weren't about to shed any light on it. I was going at it the hard way, trying to teach the colt and myself at the same time. Lige knew. He'd say, here, John, try this. it might work for you. There weren't many of those other fellas that would help a kid. They'd rather watch the wreck and laugh. Pretenders.

John

John went away to college and lost track of Lige for a while. He knew that the company partners couldn't agree on the expense of keeping Lige on the payroll and his father said that Lige had quit. But he gave it little thought until he returned home and was sorting cattle in the field next to the fairgrounds. There was Lige on his hands and knees planting petunias along the sidewalks where the carnival rides would set up.

Come fall the manager of the Bare Ranch called on Lige to show his new cow boss the country. He was a-horseback again in the country he knew as well as anyone: Buffalo Hills, Deep Hole, Grass Valley, the Granites.

*In 1964 I went to work for Bob Rodriguez at the Bare
Ranch and that fall I was camped with Lige at Grass
Valley. The outfit had bought eight head of horses from
Terry Cahill, in Warner Valley, and they were turned
over to me to ride. This big sorrel horse blew up with me
late one day. The horse could buck pretty hard and I
wasn't feeling a bit comfortable. Lige was there so quick.
He rode into the horse and got his head up. Stayed right
alongside until he quit bucking. I would've been bucked
off several times that fall if it hadn't been for him.*

*We gathered all that country, the two of us. It was get-
ting pretty late in the year but we still had some places he
wanted to look at again. We split up and agreed to meet
back in camp that afternoon or evening. I ran into some
cows and calves a long way out. They were thin and slow
and it got dark on me. It was snowing hard and I got con-
fused whether I was going the right way or not. I figured
the cattle'd work on down so I turned them loose and
headed to camp. It quit snowing and really got cold.
Finally I could make out that rock monument on the sky-
line behind camp. It was just midnight when I walked in*

the cabin. Lige said it was dark when he got in. He'd step outside ever so often to listen for me, could hear my tapaderos tapping together an hour before I got there. He had supper all cooked but hadn't eaten himself.

We finished riding and got the cattle from Lost Creek to the Bare Ranch. He stayed until the calves were weaned and everything classed up for winter, then he went to his home in Cedarville.

Ray Morgan, *buckaroo*

I first heard about Lige when I took a pair of broken reins into Charlie Pratt's saddle shop in Cedarville, in the winter of 1978. Charlie's was a hangout for the ranchers in the wintertime. He kept a coffeepot going and he didn't seem to notice the mud on their work boots. I put the rawhide reins on the counter and braced myself for a stampede of comments about "how the reins got broke" and "leppy easterners who don't know anything." In truth, I'd tied up a green horse with the reins; he pulled back and broke them. It was my own fault, but I wasn't about to admit that out loud. Charlie rolled the frayed ends in his fingers and shook his head. "I can't do a thing with these. Lige braids rawhide. Maybe he can fix 'em for you."

A few days later, my friend Nancy and I followed Charlie's directions to a dark red house on Townsend Street. I tapped on the screen door. There was shadowy figure in the kitchen, but it didn't move. I knocked harder, and the shadow stirred. The inner door creaked open a few inches. The storm door remained firmly shut. An old woman peered at us.

"What do you want?" she asked.

I told her we were looking for Lige Langston. Had we the right house?

"You those girls from Massachusetts?" she wanted to know.

Yes, we were those two girls. Did we have the right house?

"He's not here," she said firmly.

"But does he live here? Can we leave a message for him here?"

She paused for a long moment. Then she said sorrowfully,

"Haven't you heard? He's gone away . . ."

Nancy and I looked at each other helplessly. Then she took a deep breath and asked in a timorous voice, "Will he be coming back?"

The old woman snorted, "He's working at the Bare Ranch. But when he gets home, he's not going to waste his time with you." The door swung closed.

Gwendolyn Clancy, *filmmaker*

It was still cows and horses he felt in his hands.

Photo by Gwendolyn Clancy

In Town

A thing you hope for may be nearly gone before you realize you had it all along. Maybe it's because we've become a society of instruction and our sense of perception withers, but coming toward you, it can be as hard to see as a blade.

Age took its time finding Lige. He didn't appear to anticipate its meaning and went forward clearly as a child doing what he needed to do. I wonder if it ever occurred to him that one day he'd be without a ranch job. Lige would have been welcomed at the Bare Ranch cookhouse for a visit anytime, but they stopped calling on him for day work. The manager who learned the country from him had changed, and the new man was unwilling to take the risk of his age. More of his time fell to the solitary crafts of rawhiding and twisting horsehair ropes to make a living. It was still cows and horses he felt in his hands, but there was no heartbeat, no pulse.

After the day on Duck Flat I went by his house. Etta cracked the inside door but the storm door stood shut between us. The sun on her glasses denied me her eyes. Although I had telephoned earlier and Lige's pickup was in the drive, Etta made me feel I was about to have my ears scrubbed. Finally, she popped the latch and the door opened with a small sigh. I followed her through the kitchen, where the smell of coffee lingered. She pointed me toward the basement door with her chin and returned to the dishpan. I never knew her to step a foot down the rough pine stairs. Some people say it was because there were too many broncy horses and wild cattle down there for her, too many stories she had already heard, and too many memories that had no part for her to play.

The dim, cold basement opened up when his voice met me at the top. Rumbling motors on the street faded into the music of his words and the frail winter light seemed from a world far away. The room was neat and tidy and the smell was as particular as chokecherry blossoms, a blending of horses and cattle, tallow and sweat, hide and hair.

He pulled a chair from a corner for me and talked as he returned to the bosal he was finishing. His attention fell on the nail above the workbench that speared orders for riatas, bosals, reins, quirts, or horsehair macates. The orders were for more than handcraft. They were the only way we would be able to touch him someday, to capture him for as long as our hands might hold his work.

The art of rawhiding came naturally to Lige during the long bunkhouse evenings. He learned to repair his equipment with rawhide when it came apart. It was the most natural material available on a ranch. A hide could be stripped off a dead critter by slicing a knife up each side of the belly, around each leg, up the neck leaving the ears on the hide, tying the head to a post, another rope from the ears to the bumper of a truck sent in the opposite direction. Off it would come, slick as a peeled onion. Getting the hair and flesh off was a longer and more tedious process, but rawhide braiding was a practical way for Lige to keep one boot planted in his old life.

Boxes or bags of horse mane hair to be washed and picked were stacked along the stairwell. Rows of newspaper fringed with black, gray, sorrel, or white hair, ready for twisting, lay on an old bed. In the corner the winter's kindling was split and stacked. There was a grinding wheel like the one I remember riding at my grandpa's, pedaling as the wheel turned to sharpen steel and shine up fingers. Rawhide strings were separated by size and hung in bundles from the floor joists. Whole hides, scraped and stretched, stood like pictures along the wall. One was a special hide he had inherited from Frank Morgan, another buckaroo and rawhider. It came from an old jersey cow, no fat, no brands, glassy. When he braided it up he would think of Frank's strong hands kneading feather light sourdough biscuits, the way his face broke in half at a funny story, his loop that began as big as a house slipping down to close around a calf's neck in a whisper.

Rawhiding has been politely ignored as a folk craft by a world that does not know a life can be strung on a riata tightened between the equal weight of a cow and a horse. Charles Russell was probably the best at describing the perils of the cowboy life with a paintbrush and pigment, and what he painted was not the odd occasion but the every day. If the braider slipped his edging blade or ignored a blemish in the hide a strand could break and the rope fly apart. The wreck might not kill a person but it could leave some lasting tracks.

The riata is commonly braided of four continuous strings without splice, for strength. The trimmed hide is cut with a hand-held gauge, starting at the outside, following around to the center. Each strand is edged to keep it from curling and skived for thickness so the weight and size is even, end to end. The finished length is the pleasure of the roper, usually from forty-five to seventy feet, and since the braiding process takes up a third of the length of the raw strings, the bundles are a handful. They are made pliable by wrapping them in a damp cloth, then pulled down hard as they are braided, with a constant tension so the strands won't shrink and weaken when they dry. Lige could braid three feet an hour and carefully regulated the moisture of the bundles over the length of the rope. When the braiding was finished he pulled the riata through a series of holes drilled in a block of wood to smooth and gauge it a final time. Tallowed, it coiled into a rope that could equalize a small buckaroo with a critter twenty times larger in weight and determination. That's when the art shifts from the maker to the user and one creation is enlarged by another master. Arnold Rojas, *These Were the Vaqueros*, explains it: "The hondo commands the loop, the loop the coils, and the throw is decided by the way one whirls and casts." Without the experience, knowledge, and ability of the buckaroo the riata is just an attractive object of handcraft to hang on the wall. In the hands of the buckaroo the hide of the cow finds life again. The continuity is worth remembering. It is the flow of purpose the braider reveres.

Lige also twisted the soft mane hair into ropes. The hair rope is another elegant invention, using a series of strands that twist back on themselves to form a rope that can be tied onto a bosal to make a hackamore. The colors are kept separate for design and the size is determined by the stage of the horse's training.

The gear, the horse, and the open land elevate the buckaroo above what might otherwise be a lonely and lowly occupation. Ability with those elements can give a kind of immortality to those who know what it takes to become a master. Their name will sing out as a riata does when it bites into the desert air.

Along the workbench awls, punches, marlin spikes, knives, pliers, needles, and other tools were lined up by class and size in an old cartridge belt. His gauges were carved from sticks with a broken knife blade that could be adjusted for width. There was a peanut can for pencils and a notebook where he kept measurements and "recipes" beside a Philco radio I never heard playing. Lige seemed surprised at the number of orders that came in the mail. When another braider's work was brought in for repairs he looked it over carefully for variations he might try. He was in awe of good work, especially if it was the product of one of his many students; then tears of pride would splash down on his work pants.

His bridle hung over a red Folgers coffee can above his head: headstall of oiled harness leather, hammered silver coins on the cheek, rawhide reins, spade bit. The spade bit is reserved for the finished horse sensitive to the slightest pressure of the master horseman's hand. The mouthpiece is forged of sweet iron. Horses prefer the taste of sweet iron. It keeps their mouth moist, supple to the hands of the fine rider, and, in its way, assures a fine response.

Lige turned the bosal over in his hands, directing the string in a magical overlapping on itself. He braided as if he had two good eyes that shared a pinpoint of distance between them. Yet his hands stuttered slightly to find the place his one blind eye does not convey. A horse took that eye years before. It reared up, struck out against a rope, and knocked Lige to the ground. That night a sear of pain burned vision away, but it didn't stop him. There was a recurring lesson in his life – to simply make the best of it.

Lige kept track of important meetings and events coming up on a child's school slate. He was a deacon in the Community Church, and he helped the women serve dinner and wash dishes on Rotary night. His recipes for ravioli and jumbo raisin cookies are in the church cookbook, *Valley Vittles*. At funerals the old songs were never more poignant than when Lige sang in his clear voice:

> *I miss you when the campfire is burning*
> *And I wonder if you miss me too.*
> *I can see the Great Divide*
> *and the trails we used to ride –*
> *The only bit of Heaven I knew.*
> *When it's nighttime in Nevada I'm dreaming*
> *Of the old days on the desert, and you.*

The odd scrap of leather was kept to patch headstalls or become poppers on a quirt or romal. With Lige everything had a second chance to be useful. A can of his concoction to soften and dress the rawhide – tallow, Fells naphtha soap, and beeswax – hung under a single bulb with a pie tin shade. The light was the only heat in the basement. Its steady glare was directed over his hands as he worked the nearly transparent strings into place. The heel knot grew and filled in.

Scattered along the walls were photographs and calendar pictures cut free from the days he had used up. Cowboy cards sent by friends were stuck up with tacks. The illustrations could have been of his life. Twisted bodies of broncos bucked toward a rocky rim, or a buckaroo trailed a bunch of cows stringing down a canyon filled with sunset.

Lige finished the heel knot and smoothed it with a wooden mallet. He handed it to me. I had helped him drag the green hide out of his pickup and saw the work progress to a lithe, lively bosal that would be used to introduce the bridle to a young horse. Coarse, rough materials had been carefully braided into a balanced, useful thing.

*A thing you hope for may be nearly gone before
you realize you had it all along.*

Photo by Gwendolyn Clancy

For forty years she ranted like a sow when he threw his saddle in the pickup, latigo and cinches lapping over the side, followed him down back streets to see who he might visit and how long he rested his elbows on their gate, clawed onto the money as if it had a meaning and hardened to suppling strokes that touched her in the night, was buried in the churchyard in a grave of deep resentment for her rivals, who were horses and freedom on the land, but when the hallway echoed with the ring of profane silence, he sat in the evenings of the long and bitter tears.

A good-sized crowd gathered at the Nevada Historical Society in Reno one fall evening in 1985 to watch the premiere of Lige: Portrait of a Rawhide Worker, *a film documenting the life of longtime local buckaroo Lige Langston. When the film was done, hands shot up with questions, and Lige graciously agreed to come to the front of the hall and respond. As he walked up the aisle, with that distinctive hitch of a gait he'd inherited from some long-ago encounter with a bronc, he looked humble and a bit surprised at all the attention, but also quietly proud, not so much proud of what he had done, but just a quiet pride of being. The questions came respectfully and just a bit impatiently, as if the people gathered there couldn't quite comprehend this plain-speaking yet somehow elusive figure. Where was he actually born, one man wanted to know. "On a homestead out on Duck Flat," was his reply. Where exactly is Duck Flat? Lige gestured over his shoulder, "Oh, it's out to the north a ways." But how do you get there? "Well, you head up to the northeast over that first rise, and along those flats all the way to that first range of hills, and then when you see*

*Pyramid Lake you head north along the west shore and
then west again so you can climb up and hit that pass
just right. . . ." As Lige spoke his hand moved fluidly to
express the contour of the land, and it suddenly struck
me that he was describing the route according to how
you'd ride it horseback, not drive it. The audience
seemed to relax, perhaps sensing finally that this man
standing humbly before us was not really one of us, but
rather a living bridge to Nevada's old ways.*

Gwendolyn Clancy

Badger Camp

*I like to sit and wait for daylight to come. I don't want
the sun to catch me just saddling my horse.*

Chris Hansen, *Surprise Valley rancher*

I've never been so alone as Lige was at the Nevada cow camps,
day after day without the broken tones of another voice. The
longest may be an afternoon, an evening, but there's the telephone, town a few miles away, neighbors if I need them, television if I want. I rarely know the endless company of my own
making. I've spent weeks at our cow camp on Badger Mountain,
but we are a small community of ranchers, running in common,
working together. I've ridden all day without seeing another
buckaroo but knew eventually someone would come off a rim or
their dust would blow across the distance. I've never been filled
up with the landscape so familiar that I felt it pass through my
skin, knowing me completely.

After Etta's death, being alone for Lige took on a different
character. Everything changed. He was stuck in town. Even
though visitors came, called, and friends filled in, he became
angry. A reporter friend did a follow-up story to one done ten
years earlier, and he called me afterward, concerned. When I
read the article I understood. There were cuss words I had never
heard Lige speak. His words were jagged like a hunk of rawhide
that never felt his hands describe a purpose. I ached when I read
it.

*There was that awful mix-up over the bank accounts
and the will after Etta died. Lige hadn't been notified
when the probate was settled and it had been over a
year. He'd been left out of the whole thing, as if he wasn't
even in the picture. He called Don because he didn't
know what to do. Pearl and I drove up and met to meet
him at the lawyer's office in Alturas. Etta had* everything *in her name, house, car, accounts, even the
damned telephone. She left the house to Sam, her oldest
boy. Lige could live in the house till he died, but if he
remarried, he had to get out. She put it in the will! Lige
was devastated.*

Jessie

Then he had the accident. By the time he remembered the beeswax melting in a coffee can on the electric stove upstairs, it was very hot. Clapped in two pot holders he started for the back door, but in the washroom it exploded in his face. He got himself up to the hospital. When I arrived he was slumped in the chair closest to the door, his hands in gauze mittens and his face swollen with pain. I had no remedy, no words to restore him. On his back porch the paint and linoleum were blackened and blistered where the burning wax splashed. Smoke scuffed the walls clear to the ceiling.

Friends took turns with his meals. John and I picked him up for dinner each day and the winter months passed in a healing of two kinds. His old cheer returned at our table but each night he went home to a house that was quiet. Not the quiet of the brushy hills around camp. Not the deep quiet of the desert night. It was a square town lot with a lawn out front and trees planted like fence posts, all angles of yard and street and house, too many rooms, empty closets and dresser drawers, good dishes in the cupboard he'd never use, and her things packed away. Then a hairpin sweeps out from the baseboard in the bathroom and it's all wrong. It's all over.

John and I asked Lige to go with us to Badger Camp for the fall ride. He followed us, sage and alkali dust boiling in his open windows. His blue truck turned off the main road to Summit Lake, past the horse pasture, like it remembered the way.

Badger Mountain crouches over the high desert like its namesake, spread out, rounded off north, east, and south. Its bulk presses down over a water source and springs squirt through every fingered crevice, feeding the circumference equally well when there's a snowpack to perk downward.

The west is the faulting face. The top falls away from seven thousand feet, and seventy miles away the snowy peaks of the Warner Mountains in Surprise Valley stand clean against the sky. In that space between, exactly no one.

The first year I helped Alkali gather cattle I was sent across a place known as Chinatown, a flow of thick lava only a few million years old. Tubes and ribs are lightly littered with soil; enough to start some plants, but the living is restricted to the depth of the dirt. Sage, hopsage, balsam, rabbit brush, mahogany are half-height. Aspen are bonsai. Ferns cling in pouches along the damp lava walls draining west. Growth is slow and concentrates every inch to taste and taste again, to wait. It was a place out of reckoning, a birthplace of time.

Beyond Chinatown was sand again, bitterbrush, horsebrush, shadscale, and a sound. A hissing I couldn't put a face on chilled me. I knew no desert beast in possession of such an open-mouthed warning until a four-cornered pillow ruffled across the ground toward my horse. It was barely fetlock high and yet it charged. My horse, all eyes and ears and nostrils flared, had met its match in a badger's dark face, its light cape thrown loosely round its shoulders. I spurred away and jumped a bank and turned to see if it was still coming. Underneath a brush three small sets of eyes peered from a hole just as she plugged off light.

I met the one who owned the mountain.

The Alkali Cattle Company headquartered at a camp on the east side of Badger Mountain. The range was on public land, split between the Bureau of Land Management and the Charles Sheldon National Antelope Refuge. Our cows roamed over about three hundred square miles – more, before the government fencing projects of the 1970s. In those early days our cows had their favorite places and often mixed with the neighbors' cattle. We roderoed with the Virgin Valley, the MC, Soldier Meadows, Dufurrena, Frenchy Montero ranches, and our home ranch fence was the last fence east for 150 miles. Even after fences, the weather could rescue us from the government's range management techniques. A fluke storm dumped eighteen inches of snow on the last day of August 1971. When it snows in high desert country cows start looking for the feed wagon, so they packed up and headed home over the snow-filled cattle guards. By 10 a.m. the snow was gone and the cows veered off the track to graze. The mix-up took six weeks to straighten out. One morning on the edge of Long Valley I counted twenty-three ranches represented as we held rodero. I tasted the old days.

In the 1930s a Civilian Conservation Corps crew camped above the meadow and built a pretty rock cabin on the hill for the refuge. For a few years the Alkali buckaroos were allowed to use the cabin when they shipped beef at the end of summer and when they gathered the pairs in the fall, but they were asked out after it nearly burned down. The fire started after a poker game that was part liquid, part smoke, part game of chance. The game was fueled by hunters who hoped for a nudge toward an old mossback. It matured as Billy McCluskey, drunk enough to stand on the table with a winning hand, sang, "Oh, the little black bull is comin' down the mountain!" Maybe somebody's pants were thrown too close to the stove or a cigarette fell into a bedroll, smoldering until flames crackled under the bed springs. The next spring the Alkali buckaroos built their own cabin closer to the corrals.

John and I didn't know it then but fall had come for us, too. In a few short months we'd stand on the west faulting face of our lives. The ag loan company that had handed out money like feed store calendars would react to the panic of the mid-1980s, reverse themselves, and want it back. Bank officers would sit at our table and I would put out coffee and cake, as if for guests. They would examine our neat ledgers, using words I wouldn't understand and eyes I would. When the talk was done a notice would come in our mailbox. The postmistress would point to the line where I was to sign for it and turn away. Ask me anything about that day and I can tell it. I remember it all like a bone remembers where it was broken.

John and I would saddle up our horses and ride the circle, gathering the range, and in a dream that would not end, the cows would disappear into the brush ahead, no dust, no tracks, not even the smell we knew was cow. Dozens of trucks would roll up the snow-plowed road, diesel engines throb the window glass as they passed by the house. We would push every one of our desert cows up the chute, then, side by side, stand in the lane watching them go.

Saddle horses fat as brood mares would stand idle pulling stems of hay down from the rack. We would look out at our empty fields and decide what it is we are. If we were not ranchers we would know it then.

And finally another truck would come our way, past the house to the chute, and unload one Hereford heifer carrying our brand, mixed in a neighbor's cattle, separated out and returned. One heifer. Ridiculous. We would open the gate. She would walk into the snow-covered meadow and, looking all around for other cows, she would bawl, her icy breath hanging in the air.

The first time I saw the black horse he was standing by a fence south of Badger Camp near Mitchell Troughs. His long mane twisted in witch knots, his tail a wad. Scars healed in peppery gray hair on the black like sweat dried. He leaned his chest against the wire as if he'd found himself on the wrong side. Bright blood bathed the barbs and beaded the dust between his front feet.

I thought about the black horse from time to time. Maybe because he was alone. Maybe because he leaned his chest so hard on the wire.

I didn't see him for about a year. He'd found a way across the fence and was deep in the crease of a canyon, no other horses around. An old range stud that had been whipped away from his band by a young challenger. He grazed the rocky sidehill toward a pocket of bitterbrush.

Drought settled on the basin again that year as it would for eight years. Children would be born and go to school never knowing their home landscape wasn't supposed to be so leached of tender growth, so brittle, so harsh, so dry. As a community we were linked in a poverty of rainfall, compressed by endurance. Those years hovered over us in a shadow of the desert's wing. We refused to say its name.

It's well we didn't know at the onset. The meadows grew silent as geese, cranes, blackbirds, early robins migrated on another route and the whistle of swans ran high and swift through the night sky above us. But it laid on one day at a time. That was its power over us. The historic record proved drought's domination over this region for thousands of years, scouring life from its face. Hope was a wavering light. I feared we would never see the hunch of bully thunderheads on the western peaks or mare's tails sweep red skies of dawn with a warning for sailors of the great inland sea to dock our boats of sand.

The artesians were the first to dry up as neighboring wells were drilled or deepened or pumped around the clock. The ground around them subsided, scuffed with the cracks and scabs of drought. Plants curled into themselves just as we did. Pastures were bare as the barnyard. We cut back on numbers and hauled water to stock waiting at the tanks. The lakes dried up. Their salts blew above the valley in clouds that seemed never to settle back down.

We'd drive out on the playa at night, stop the jeep, walk out a distance, and lay our backs on its flatness. Not knowing what else to do, we opened our eyes to the night and asked what wisdom required such suffering. There was no reply.

In the canyon of the black horse lupine, mule ears, paint-brush grew spindly, the future trusted to fewer seeds. Grass crowns crunched and powdered. Cow trails deepened, sand to gravel, gravel to mud, mud to murky pools. I never saw the horse all summer.

When we rode the foothills that winter we came on deer after deer, sprawled dead in the brush. They'd migrated according to their habit, chewed stems of drought-killed browse and willow limbs until they packed their guts with starvation. It was not just deer. Rabbits disappeared. Quail came cautiously into the calf lot for oats and rye that leaked through the feeder and drank at the trough. One of the dogs packed in a coyote skull and lay by the shop gnawing the scalp off.

That's why, come spring, I was surprised to see the black horse alive, grazing along with a bunch of cows in the saddle of the pass, and right then I knew rain would come. I saw him by the wire. I saw him by the water. I saw him in the spring. I would see him always.

While the men unloaded the horses from stock trailers, I drove up the hill to put the food away and straighten the cabin. The key to the padlock was on the hook in the old screenside cooler under the north eaves, as usual. A Lysol wash and supper cooking would chase out stale air and the smell of mice inside. As I built a fire in the cook stove to heat wash water a golden marmot sat on the step watching me, measuring his whiskers one side at a time, both paws working together.

I tried to imagine how it was when Lige worked for Alkali and lived in these rooms for half a year, alone, the kerosene lamps burning their tart perfume, their light punching a hole in the darkness. After supper was put away and his braiding laid aside, the door would be left standing open, moonlight leaning as one bright wedge into this room where night lay beside him on the cot.

I sliced three big white onions and let them go transparent in the skillet while I took a pan of potatoes and the peeler out to the porch. It was a job I did at my sink nearly every night in a rush between the last job and next. There I was on the stoop, as if I had all the time in the world, as if peeling a pan of potatoes born of dark earth and silence was the only thing I wanted to do.

Down the hill some of the men were carrying saddles and sacks of grain into the saddle shed while John and Bill shod the horses tied in the round corral. With each sharp ring I knew the steel shoe was bending on the edge of the harder anvil. The duller thud was the hammer sinking the nail. Voices lifted and settled as the day had done.

It was nearly dark when they came walking up the road, two by two, like old horses, one in each wheel track worn through the wire grass. They sat on the battered couch outside, taking turns at the washbowl, sleeves rolled up but water-stained, and some around the neck and front. Their talk was heavy with home still clinging to it: haying in the fields alone, broken-down machinery, repairs, grease, getting the most out of every acre, of every drop of water, of every hour in every day, of every dollar. It took time to step out of the harness of home and relearn the lessons of the desert.

They came inside to help with supper. Someone set the table, dealing out plates like poker cards, and we moved around each other in the small kitchen the easy way a family can.

After supper and the dishes Lige walked outside. When I threw the dishwater from the basin I could see him standing, listening to the spring pipe letting go of the water, and the water talking its way to the meadow. Stars stood out against the night like signal fires, Orion's belt still holding them together for me. The moon rested on the mahoganies along the dark ridge and its reflection swam in the water tank. I scooped her up. For just a moment I held the moon in my hands.

You are taking the sunshine
that has brightened my path for a while.

Photo by Gwendolyn Clancy

End of Summer, 1997

John dropped the fence pliers in the sand and lifted the water jug. He looked down the fence line a mile to the corner where we left Lige's truck at sunup. After Lige died, we bought his GMC truck – bumper sticker of a cowboy making a good ride on a wild saddle bronc and in bright red letters, LET'S RODEO! – little quirt still suspended from the keys.

When our saddle horses get too old for work we drive them to a field by the lake. They graze fine-stemmed grass all summer and seek shade in an old grove of black willows. Lithe branches swipe flies away. Leaves whisper in their sleep. Sweet water rises from an iron pipe, splashes brightly into a trough, out the overflow, soaking back into the ground. The soil is sandy. Easy on their flinty hooves. Easy digging.

I could not have endured Lige waking to played-out days in the old folks home, feeling the way an orphan must, cut off from the comfort of home, habit, neighbors, church, community. Pictures of the family thumbtacked to corkboard don't change the temporary lodgings.

New patients get broke to the hospital schedule the same way a colt leaves the herd and learns the ways of compromise.

They cooperate, wait their turn, eat what's put before them, trade freedom for ease. Patients are encouraged to ride wheelchairs to meals, tests, and activities instead of shank's mare. A wheelchair can be a fast horse on a short track, an old-age banana peel. They live according to a file folder that describes what they are and how they are. But not who.

On a winter day I drove to the long-term care facility in Alturas to visit some of the people I had taped for the historical society. I had entered their lives asking them to speak of their most personal memories. They willingly gave me confidence and friendship. I couldn't just walk away.

O. D. Van Norman, a 104-year-old former cow boss, buckaroo boss, and Indian fighter, was not in his room. An empty room always made me apprehensive. I asked at the nurse's station. She pointed down the hall to the activities room. Wheelchairs were parked around the dining room like used cars on a lot. Old faces smiled at me eager for company or stared into a private space where a clock ticks but the hands don't move.

Van's wheelchair was by the front window. He was watching a young woman get three little boys out of a car and into the dentist's office. He chuckled. "I tried to herd hogs once when I was a kid and it looked just like that."

A cocky orderly stepped between us and "Hee-Haw" style said, "We're gonna have us a ro-dee-o, ain't we, old-timer!" He plopped a child's cowboy hat on Van's head. It was a cheap little hat made of red wool felt, stitched with white lacing around the brim. He wheeled Van around to a little wooden rocking horse and called out, "Gather round, folks. This here cowboy's gonna show us how to rope a wild horse. How 'bout it, Pop?" He stuck a limp lariat made of clothesline in Van's hand. Van looked over at me.

I'd like to tell you that Van swung the loop around his head several smart spins, pitched it at the orderly's head, jerked his slack, dallied around the armrest, and laid his spurs to the flanks of his wheelchair. I want to say that the orderly yelped as he skidded along behind that wild, raging cowboy. But that's not what happened.

Van just flipped the loop side-handed. It took on air like a piece of wet spaghetti and flopped down short of the target.

"Oh, oh!" The orderly laughed. "I guess that wild horse got away, Pop."

"Don't call me Pop!" Van growled and wheeled solemnly back to his room. The rope lay on the tile floor with his memories of horses and buckaroos on the high desert cow country. None of it was any use to him now.

Lige was in the best place to die. At Jessie's. She made breakfast for him as the sun came up low in its winter arc, reflected on the December snow, slicing through the bare limbs of the elm to ignite the apricot jam in its crystal dish. She set their plates on the table, eggs sunny side up, bacon, toast, cups of coffee trailing steam into the light, and she looked toward the hall, listening.

The night before, he shoveled the walk while she took care of the chickens. Together they carried the little potted spruce into the living room. Normally she kept the folk's tradition of trimming the tree on Christmas Eve but Lige was driving home the next day. She decided to go ahead with it while he was still there and let their celebration carry her through the last week of

Advent. She told him she wanted to decorate the tree simple like they did on the Flat, with strings of popcorn and rosehips and sprigs of pungent sage. They made two bowls of popcorn, one to string for the tree and one for them to eat while they worked. He stood beside her at the organ and they sang the Christmas songs Pearl had taught them, the songs the Salvation Army soldiers sang on the streets of Reno at holiday time, songs that held them together as a family. Their voices were a harmony of the garlands draped crisscross, bough to bough.

Jessie rose at six, as usual. When she walked from her room to the kitchen an hour earlier Lige was in the bathroom and the door was standing open. His reflection smiled from the mirror as he shaved. He winked. She hadn't realized how much she missed the smell of a man's shaving soap in her house. Old Spice. Opaque bottle. The ship's rigging billowed with the wind of faith: the earth is round, a safe port lies open to the sea.

He opened his valise, put his extra shirt on top the toiletry case, buckled the straps, and set the case by the bedroom door. As he straightened up the room darkened and a pressure filled his head. His heart froze open. Suddenly past center, hands still at his side, Lige fell face down on the floor. Silence followed back down the wire. Jessie didn't hear because she wasn't there. But she knew.

The wires pulled tight against juniper posts John's grandfather had tamped solid long before John was born. He put his hand on the post and tried to rock it but it stood as if it had grown there. "You know, things just don't rot in this old alkali ground."

John lifted the green jug and bubbles passed upward, breaking through the water. He handed the jug to me, then wiped his mouth on his sleeve. We would finish the fence today and, tomorrow morning, trail our dry cows across the lake. They could winter on the dry feed in the hot springs field on a tenth of the hay cows with calves need.

It's just John and me now. No hired men. Kay died on Memorial Day from the effects of a devastating stroke she suffered four years earlier. My dad passed away. Mom and Walter are adjusting to living alone I suppose, though I doubt a person ever gets used to living by half. Mom's still raising horses on their home place at the foot of Diablo Mountain. Walter works in the shop, picks up the tools we scatter around the flanks of the baler, swather, and bale wagon, and has the advice we need. When we sold our cows in the 1980s John never took a backward step. He led the partnership from that point on. Our assets were a couple of old tractors, some tired haying equipment, the land, and our ability. We took a contract to calve out 250 first calf heifers the first year, raised 300 drop calves for a dairy the second year, cut our expenses every year, took in pasture cattle for the grass season, chopped hay and fed some through the winter, held onto our ranch flock, sold some land, and worked toward being debt-free for the first time in our lives. I would guess most ag operations move on the grease of borrowed money, and without that latitude we realize growth by the loving inch. This year we had calf crop enough to ask friends for help with the branding. Some of the calves trace back to that single Hereford heifer returned on that snowy day. We sold our permit on the Sheldon the Hussas had held since the 1930s. We're not on the desert anymore. That's a deep regret. At times it was hard to see the positive in the change forced on us, especially selling a part of the ranch. I'd go back to conversations I had with Lige. His life was spent on the land, not owning it, and doing his work. Every day.

I pulled two apples from my coat pocket and we sat down on a sandy knoll.

"John, did you know Francine?"

"Sure. You'd see her, Neva Lowell, and my grandmother at the Cozy Corner all the time. Every Sunday for sure. She always looked pretty and real trim. Anytime you saw her in town she had her makeup on and her hair fixed up, always. Classy. Old Moose Erramouspe moved her little trailer house on his property sometime in the '50s. I used to drive by their place on the way to school and she'd be out working in the garden. They lived like that for years. Keeping up appearances."

"Erramouspe? Was he related to the Erramouspe killed in Little High Rock Canyon?"

"His son. Moose. He was a real decent guy. Worked up at the mill for years. When Herman Johnson started up the airport, he took up flying. They had quite a bunch in their club. Most of 'em had been pilots in the war."

"Why did they call him Moose?"

"Oh, Honey. He looked like one. He had the biggest Basco nose you ever saw. His name was John but they tagged Moose on him when he was a kid. He was always Moose to everybody."

"Whatever happened to Francine?"

"She died right before you came up to this country. Did you know that Lige sang at her funeral?"

"No. I had no idea. Do you remember what he sang?"

"'Red River Valley,' I imagine. It was an old favorite of his." He brushed the sand beside him in a sweep like a fan, twin to those made by weeds the wind pushes about, taproot tried but twisted down and holding on.

"I don't think they ever stopped loving each other." He took an apple from me and rubbed it slowly on his pants leg.

"Maybe I'm finally starting to figure things out. The other night Lavelle said something that's been bo'thering me. 'If it hadn't been for Etta, Lige wouldn't have had anything.' At first I thought, she doesn't know what she's talking about, but by golly, she might be right.

"I watched Lige when I rode with him at Badger. He could take any kind of horse and if he needed to he could drop a loop on a big old cow and his horse would drag her wherever he wanted to go. He was not one of those guys that wore a diamond horseshoe pinkie ring. He was interested in getting the work done and he rode the horse he was on.

"Lavelle made me remember something Jessie told me once. She said, 'Women liked Lige but they said they didn't see any future in what he was doing.' When Lige married Etta he was riding free, working hard, living hard. He knew the cow business, but Etta understood the dollar. She looked to the future. Together they developed their ranch and for the first time in his life Lige had something besides a saddle and a bedroll.

"I think Lige saw Etta honestly and tolerated her shortcomings because he credited her that he didn't end up doing day work on somebody's ranch, living out his life in a bunkhouse." John reached over and tucked a stand of hair behind my ear. His finger traced the curve, jawline to chin. "I always wished he had a wife he could be a partner with, but he just didn't. He had Etta."

He took my hand and pulled me to my feet. Then he gathered up the fence pliers and can of staples. I carried the water jug and what was left of the wire. His free arm round my shoulder. We went on down the line.

Afterword

Lige Langston received a national honor when the Smithsonian Institution in Washington, D.C., requested samples of his rawhide braiding and horsehair ropes to be placed for permanent displays in the archives. He is the subject of a documentary film, *Lige: Portrait of a Rawhide Worker,* winner of Best Ethnographic Film at the UCLA Film Folklore Festival.

I met Lige in 1971. He was working for the Bare Ranch, doing the same work that had been his life's habit. From spring turnout until the end of the cow work in the fall, Lige stayed at the ranch in a room in the main house, eating in the cookhouse with the other buckaroos, returning to Cedarville on the weekend. During the winter Lige took up his rawhiding and visiting. It was a rare day there was not a car or pickup parked in front of the house. Students, customers, buckaroos, braiders – friends came in a steady flow.

My recorded conversations with Lige began as a part of the Modoc County oral history program. Because of our friendship and shared love of ranch work and life, the interviews expanded. He spoke directly to me over nearly twenty years of his work, family, and friends – I'm faithful to him on that – but never of his personal affairs with women. I never heard him say the name Francine. He never said he was married to her or divorced from her. I don't know how long they were married but was told it was brief. His second marriage, to Etta Harris, lasted forty-two years.

Lige's sisters, Jessie Langston Holmes, Margaret Langston Bariski, and Pearl Langston MacDonald, and friends – Buze Miller, Ray Morgan, Dick Winnop, Buster Dollarhide, Pete Crystal, Sydney Harris, Lavelle Stevens Dollarhide, Jimmie Washoe, Fern Jones Gooch, Kay Gooch Hussa, Charlie Van Norman, Philip Van Norman, Bill Heryford, Bill Cockrell, Gwen Clancy, Nancy Kelly, Mike Semenario, Pete Ytciana, and "the town gossip" – spoke to me about Lige and the two women who shared his life. Their stories form those chapters. I was acquainted with Etta for many years. When I went to see Lige she shortstopped me in the kitchen, showed me pictures of her grandchildren, but I can't say I knew her.

Etta is buried in the Eagleville cemetery with her first husband, Arthur Harris, the father of her two sons.

Lige is buried in a single plot in the Cedarville cemetery. His grave is in the front row and faces east, where the sun speaks first as it rises over the mountains of Nevada.

Resting

I could not bear the dirt
clods broken apart one from the other
angry, wholly forlorn.
It was not the fertile ground a plow opens
before the drill files round, giving
seeds parting from the hull
capillaries tender reach – no.
A plot – the size of a man
laid out, sleeping, gaining strength
to rise up and work on.

Valley quail scratch the dirt for grit.
A meadowlark loops to the marker post,
gold larynx flared in intricate song.
Friends come and stand.

 Rocks began to appear on the grave
shortly after the ground healed up
 – hard flecked chunks from Granite Mountain,
Stone Corral's pink cream chert,
the gauze of Empire's gypsum,
petrified wood from Badger, smooth
agate rolled down Tuledad Wash.
What else could we bring?

 Tangled in the rocks is a wild rose
that might be found in the desert anywhere
 – sweet pink flowers, thorns,
scarlet hips. Seeds.

319

Acknowledgments

True to the way we live here in Surprise Valley, this book was a community effort. People stopped me in front of the post office and without my even asking them began talking about Lige. We'd sit down on the bench, someone else would come by headed inside for the mail and would hunker down beside us. Often it was just the right story, one I didn't even know I wanted. John and I are both richer for this experience.

Many books and newspapers were important in my research. *The Last Free Man* by Dayton O. Hyde, *Frozen Grass* by Kenneth D. Scott, *The Indian Massacre of 1911* by Effie Mona Mack, the *New Era, Humboldt Star, Humboldt Sun, Reno Evening Gazette, Surprise Valley Journal,* and *Range Magazine* were useful in the reconstruction of the incident in Little High Rock Canyon. *The Road to Reno* by Nelson Manfred Blake put the history of divorce in Nevada into a perspective of time and social change. *These Were the Vaqueros* by Arnold R. Rojas explained terminology and tradition brought to the region by the Californios.

My thanks to the following publishers for their permission to print poems that appear here in a form altered from the original work: "The Horse Runner," from *Where the Wind Lives,* Gibbs Smith; "For Forty Years" and "Once in a Blue Moon," from *Ride the Silence,* Black Rock Press. Additional passages previously appeared in another form published by *Great Basin Magazine* and *Dry Crik Review.*

My thanks to dear friends for their advice critical to the development of the manuscript: Catie Webster, Dawn Marano, Sophie Sheppard, Charlie Buck, Katie Hussa Tims, Jean Dunnington, Nancy Kelly, Gary Short, Gwendolyn Clancy, Laurie Wagner Buyer, Anne Heath Widmark, Betty and Snooks Smith, and Linda Dufurrena; to editors Kimberly Wiar, Alice Stanton, and Larry Hamberlin for sharing the vision of Lige; to Jean Dunnington, my guiding spirit; and to William Kittredge, who was raised in Warner Valley, sister to Surprise as Duck Flat is sister to the south, and knows it as home to good people like Lige.